# The Unbound Lawyer

## Integrity, Justice and Professional Excellence in Practice

**Dr John McSwiney**

https://www.timetotransform.world

McSwiney, John (author)
Title: *The Unbound Lawyer: Integrity, Justice and Professional Excellence in Practice*/ Dr John McSwiney, author.
Illustrations: Canva

ISBN: 978-1-7643962-3-3

Law › Legal Education
Law › Ethics & Professional Responsibility
Business & Economics › Professional Practice
Business & Economics › Leadership & Motivation
Education & Teaching › Higher & Continuing Education
Psychology › Applied Psychology
Self-Help › Personal Transformation

The Unbound Series

Dedication

# DEDICATION

**To the Quiet Work**

For those who do the work quietly,

hold the weight without recognition,

and remain faithful to justice, one decision at a time.

# AT THE THRESHHOLD

The cover of *The Unbound Lawyer* is deliberately restrained. The deep navy blue background reflects the seriousness of the profession, a colour long associated with authority, responsibility, and trust. Navy carries weight without aggression. It signals stability rather than spectacle, discipline rather than display. It is the colour of institutions that endure. At the centre of the cover stands a solitary figure, rendered in black and white. The figure is intentionally anonymous. There is no face, no defining feature, no expression to interpret. This is not a portrait of any one lawyer, but a reflection of many. It allows the reader to see themselves in the image without instruction or expectation. The figure stands within a room of near-total darkness. This darkness is not a judgment. It represents the cumulative weight of legal practice, complexity, pressure, moral ambiguity, and the unseen emotional labour that accompanies responsibility over time. It is the space lawyers often inhabit quietly, without language or acknowledgement.

Ahead of the figure is an open door. The door is not dramatic. It is not ornate. It is simply open. From the other side, light enters the room and falls upon the figure. The light does not erase the darkness behind them. It illuminates just enough to allow a step forward. This is intentional. In law, clarity rarely arrives as certainty. It arrives as discernment, sufficient light to act responsibly, even when the full path is not yet visible. The figure does not rush forward. They stand at the threshold. This moment, between darkness and light, between habit and choice, between endurance and discernment, reflects the central question of the book: *how will you practise when pressure is constant and consequence is real?* The open door represents possibility, but also responsibility. To step through is to practise differently, not by abandoning the law, but by entering it with greater awareness, integrity, and care.

The cover contains no legal symbols. No gavels. No scales. No books. This omission is deliberate. *The Unbound Lawyer* is not about the mechanics of law, but about the person entrusted to practise it. The image does not promise ease. It offers orientation. It reflects the premise of this book: that practising law unbound is not a departure from seriousness, but a deeper commitment to it. It is the choice to step forward with clarity rather than habit, conscience rather than reactivity, and integrity rather than erosion.

The door is open.

The step is yours.

The Unbound Series

Contents

# CONTENTS


| | | |
|---|---|---|
| | Dedication | 3 |
| | Front Cover: At the Threshold | 4 |
| | Contents | 6 |
| | Acknowledgements | 8 |
| | Personal Message from Dr John | 9 |
| | Professional Assurance – A Note For Lawyers | 11 |
| | Your Unbound Leader Oath | 14 |
| | How to use this Book | 16 |
| | Introduction | 19 |
| **Part 1** | **The Lawyer Behind The Role** | **22** |
| | Module 1 – Breathing | 25 |
| | Module 2 – I Am… | 37 |
| | Module 3 - Mirror | 49 |
| | Module 4 - Grounding | 61 |
| **Part 2** | **Move Into Excellence in Practice** | **77** |
| | Module 5 – Neuroinguistics | 80 |
| | Module 6 – Compassion | 94 |
| | Module 7 – Listening | 108 |
| | Module 8 – Focus | 122 |
| **Part 3** | **Return to Purpose and the Human Meaning of Law** | **136** |
| | Module 9 - Forgiveness | 139 |
| | Module 10 – Kindness | 155 |

| | |
|---|---|
| Module 11 - Reflection | 169 |
| Module 12 - Homecoming | 188 |
| What Comes Next – Living and Practising Unbound | 202 |
| You Are Not Alone | 206 |
| Your Unbound Journey Series | 209 |
| Continue your Unbound Journey | 211 |
| Closing Note | 212 |
| Continuing Professional Development (CPD) – Professional Use Statement | 213 |
| About The Author | 216 |

# ACKNOWLEDGMENTS

This book was shaped by people and experiences far beyond its pages. I am grateful to the many colleagues across private practice, government, education, and defence who have worked alongside me over the years. Some offered guidance, some challenge, some quiet example. All, in different ways, revealed what integrity looks like when pressure is real and consequence unavoidable. I have learned as much from observing how law and governance is practised as from studying what it requires. I acknowledge the students I have had the privilege to teach. Teaching law has consistently deepened my understanding of practice. I am thankful to the clients who placed their trust in me at moments of vulnerability and uncertainty. Their stories are a reminder that law is never abstract to those it serves. The responsibility they entrust to lawyers is both a privilege and a weight, and this book exists in part to honour that trust. I also acknowledge those within the profession who are quietly doing the work well, without recognition, without fanfare, and often without language for the load they carry. This book is written with you in mind. Finally, I am grateful for the conversations - formal and informal, that challenged my assumptions and sharpened my thinking. This work did not emerge from certainty, but from reflection, practice, and the willingness to sit with complexity rather than resolve it too quickly. Any clarity found in these pages belongs to those who shaped it. Any shortcomings remain my own.

# PERSONAL MESSAGE FROM DR JOHN

If you are holding this book, it is likely because you care deeply about the law, and perhaps because you are feeling the weight of practising it. I have written this book as a practising lawyer, an academic, and, above all, as a fellow human being who knows what it means to carry responsibility over time. I know the discipline the profession demands, the precision it requires, and the quiet toll it can take when pressure becomes constant and space for reflection disappears. This book did not emerge from a belief that lawyers need fixing. On the contrary, it emerged from respect, for the intelligence, commitment, and ethical seriousness I have witnessed across private practice, government, education, and defence. It also emerged from an awareness that even the most capable lawyers can find themselves stretched thin, operating on competence alone, and slowly losing connection with the deeper reasons they entered the profession. I believe strongly that the law matters. I also believe that the people who practise it matter just as much.

*The Unbound Lawyer* is not an argument for doing less, caring less, or stepping away from responsibility. It is an invitation to practise with greater clarity, steadiness, and care, to remain whole in a profession that often rewards self-suppression in the name of performance. Everything in this book has been shaped by lived experience: by matters that did not resolve cleanly, by decisions made without certainty, by conversations that required restraint rather than force, and by moments when reflection mattered more than speed. It has also been shaped by teaching and learning alongside students, colleagues, and peers who continue to challenge how we think about professionalism, ethics, and justice. If this book offers anything of value, I hope it is permission permission to pause, to reflect, and to practise with conscience as well as competence. Permission to recognise that strength does not require hardness, and that clarity is often found not by pushing harder, but by returning to what matters.

You will not find prescriptions here. You will find practices. You will not find answers neatly resolved. You will find questions worth sitting with. Take what serves you. Leave what does not. Return when the work feels heavy, or when clarity feels distant. Above all, know this: you are not alone in this profession, even when it feels that way. Many lawyers are quietly navigating the same terrain, holding the same tensions, and asking the same questions, often without language for them. It is my hope that this book meets you not as an instruction, but as a companion, steady, respectful, and grounded in the realities of the work you do. Thank you for the work you carry. Thank you for the care you bring to it, and thank you for continuing to practise with integrity in a profession that depends upon it.

- **Dr John McSwiney**

# PROFESSIONAL ASSURANCE - A NOTE FOR LAWYERS

When you engage with a book in the **Unbound Series**, you are not engaging with a personal development text in the conventional sense. You are engaging with a **structured, evidence-informed professional framework** designed to support ethical judgment, reflective practice, and sustainable performance across demanding professional contexts, including the practice of law. The Unbound framework has been deliberately aligned with recognised Australian learning and professional standards, including the **Australian Qualifications Framework (AQF)**, the **Australian Skills Quality Authority (ASQA)** standards, the **National Safety and Quality Health Service (NSQHS) Standards**, and the **Australian Public Sector Integrated Leadership System (ILS)**.

This alignment is intentional. It ensures that the reflective and practical work invited in these pages is **legitimate, measurable, and transferable**, rather than abstract or anecdotal. The growth supported here is grounded in the same principles of quality, rigour, and ethical responsibility that underpin Australia's most trusted education, governance, and professional systems. For lawyers, this matters. It means that practices such as reflection, emotional regulation, ethical discernment, and conscious communication are treated not as personal preferences or wellbeing add-ons, but as **professional capabilities** directly relevant to judgment, conduct, and fitness to practise. The Unbound methodology is designed to translate qualities often discussed informally, clarity, compassion, restraint, integrity, into **recognised, assessable professional competencies**.

## THE EVIDENCE BASE

At the centre of this professional assurance sits ***Time to Transform: Living Unbound – The Evidence Companion***, which provides the scholarly and analytical foundation for the entire Unbound ecosystem. Developed from a thirty-module emotional intelligence and wellbeing program delivered between 2024 and 2025, the Evidence Companion supplies the academic architecture and evaluation framework that supports professional, institutional, and peer-reviewed application. Where the Unbound books invite reflection and integration, the Evidence Companion provides the **evidence base** that legitimises those practices. The Evidence Companion comprises thirty analytical essays, one corresponding to each *Living Unbound* practice, integrating theory, neuroscience, and applied professional insight. Collectively, these essays:

- map emotional, ethical, and leadership competencies to national frameworks (AQF, ASQA, NSQHS, APS ILS)
- integrate findings from neuroscience, psychology, and leadership studies into applied professional practice
- provide implementation tools, fidelity considerations, and evaluation measures (including WHO-5, PANAS, PSS-10, and optional HRV methodologies)
- offer logic models, data rubrics, and reporting templates to support transparent, accountable delivery

This material is designed to ensure that Unbound programs can be delivered, evaluated, and reviewed with the level of scrutiny expected in professional and regulatory environments.

## WHAT THIS ALIGNMENT DOES, AND DOES NOT, CLAIM

This alignment does **not** imply endorsement by any regulator or professional body. It does, however, establish **professional legitimacy**. It confirms that the learning outcomes and practices embedded in the Unbound Series reflect the same competencies sought in capable professionals across law, governance, education, and public service: ethical judgment, reflective capacity, emotional regulation under pressure, responsible use of authority, and sustainable professional conduct. For lawyers, each Unbound title functions as both **mirror and manual**, inviting reflection while offering structured ways to integrate insight into daily practice. The work is designed to support CPD engagement, professional reflection, and long-term fitness to practise without straying into therapeutic or clinical domains.

## A FINAL WORD

Choosing to engage with the Unbound framework is not a declaration of self-improvement. It is a commitment to **professional seriousness**, to practising with clarity, integrity, and care in environments where consequence is real and pressure is constant. This is development with standards. Reflection with rigour. Humanity held within professional discipline. The Unbound Series offers a continuum of evidence-informed, ethically grounded professional practice, where growth is accountable, judgment is strengthened, and the lawyer's humanity is treated not as a liability, but as a professional responsibility.

**Welcome to the Unbound Series.**

The Unbound Series

Oath

# YOUR UNBOUND LAWYER OATH

The choice of an oath, rather than a rule, policy, or professional standard, is intentional. An oath cannot be legislated, enforced, audited, or revoked. It must be freely chosen. It does not sit within codes or compliance frameworks, but within conscience. It is not held in statute, but in truth, integrity, and the quiet authority of the heart. This is not a promise made to the profession, the court, or to others. It is a personal covenant, a commitment made in private, carried in public, and lived through practice. It cannot be measured by billable hours, outcomes, or external reward. It is measured only by alignment: between who you are, how you practise, and why you serve. By taking this oath, you acknowledge that the highest standards of law cannot be reduced to technical mastery alone. They must be embodied. Justice must be lived, not merely argued. Ethics must be breathed, not merely cited. Integrity must be renewed each day at the intersection of duty and discernment, authority and humility, reason and restraint.

This is not a contract of performance. It is a commitment to consciousness. It is a pledge to practise law with presence, moral clarity, and strength of heart, to remain human in a system that often rewards detachment, and principled in moments that test resolve. The Unbound Lawyer Oath is a reminder that transformation in law does not occur through words on a page, but through daily choice: the discipline of self-reflection, the courage of ethical restraint, and the quiet power of kindness exercised with intention. When you speak this oath, you stand alongside a growing community of lawyers, advocates, judges, academics, and legal leaders who are choosing to practise differently. Professionals who understand that precision without compassion is incomplete, and authority without integrity is fragile. Together, you become part of a movement redefining what it means to succeed in law, where excellence is balanced with empathy, where advocacy is guided by conscience, and where service to justice includes care for the self who serves it. This is not the beginning of a book. It is the beginning of a lifelong conversation between law and humanity, power and presence, judgment and wisdom. Each decision, reflection, and act of courage deepens that dialogue. To practise law unbound is not to abandon rigour or responsibility, it is to reclaim their highest expression.

## YOUR OATH

I, ________________________________________________, on this day, choose to practise law with my heart unbound.

1. I commit to honouring the wisdom of my conscience, and to trusting it as my truest compass in judgment, advocacy, and decision-making.
2. I promise to practise with courage and integrity, even when doing so is inconvenient, unpopular, or personally costly.
3. I vow to meet myself, my clients, my colleagues, and the court with compassion, recognising that kindness is not weakness, but a disciplined expression of justice.
4. I commit to reflection and restraint, ensuring that clarity, not reactivity, guides my conduct and counsel.
5. I promise to remain grounded in gratitude and humility, recognising that both success and failure are teachers in the shaping of wisdom.
6. I will embrace vulnerability as a professional strength, the foundation of trust, authenticity, and ethical leadership.
7. I vow to remain fully present in my work, engaging not only with outcomes, but with people, process, and consequence.
8. I commit to continual growth, knowing that each heart-aligned choice strengthens the integrity of the profession and the justice it serves.

This is my **Unbound Lawyer Oath**, a covenant to practise law with awareness, authenticity, courage, and compassion. To hold authority responsibly, to serve justice faithfully, and to remain unbound in every act of legal practice.

The Unbound Series

How To

# HOW TO USE THIS BOOK

**The Unbound Lawyer** is not written to be consumed. It is written to be lived. This is not a book about the law you already know. It is a book about the person who practises it, the one who carries other people's stories, holds conflict, walks into urgency, and is expected to remain sharp, composed, and certain. This book is a professional reset. A return to the deeper practice beneath the practice. Across the Unbound Series, one truth remains: **your work can only be as clear as the self who performs it.** When your nervous system is overwhelmed, your judgment narrows. When your identity becomes fused with outcomes, your resilience fractures. When your conscience is exhausted, your compassion becomes performative or disappears altogether. The Unbound Lawyer restores the foundation: **Self. Practice. Purpose.** Not as theory, as a daily discipline. Here is how to make the most of it.

**1. Begin With the Lawyer Behind the Role**

**(Time to Transform: Living Unbound - Chapters 1 Breathing • 3 I Am… • 5 Mirror • 11 Grounding)**

Start here when you feel pressured, reactive, depleted, or disconnected. These chapters return you to the inner steadiness that precedes good counsel. They strengthen the lawyer you are **before** you draft, advise, negotiate, or appear. Use this section when you are navigating:

- high stakes matters and relentless deadlines
- courtroom nerves, performance pressure, or imposter thoughts
- conflict fatigue, vicarious trauma, or emotional overload
- perfectionism, people-pleasing, or the need to control outcomes

This is where you rebuild the *internal authority* that makes external authority trustworthy.

**2. Move Into Excellence in Practice**

**(Time to Transform: Living Unbound - Chapters 14 Neurolinguistics • 15 Compassion • 25 Listening • 26 Focus)**

This section is where your craft becomes conscious. The best lawyers are not only intelligent, they are **present**. They hear what is unsaid. They choose language that de-escalates, clarifies, and persuades. They remain focused under noise and pressure. They use power responsibly. Use these chapters when you need to:

- negotiate, mediate, influence, or persuade without force
- handle difficult clients, opposing counsel, or workplace tension
- communicate with clarity under stress
- protect concentration and performance in a fragmented world

Here, you shift from practising by habit to practising by intention, from reaction to mastery.

**3. Return to Purpose, and the Human Meaning of Law**

**(Time to Transform: Living Unbound - Chapters 10 Forgiveness • 28 Reflection • 29 Homecoming • 12 Kindness)**

Law is a profession of consequence. It can shape lives, protect dignity, and restore fairness, but it can also harden the heart if the lawyer forgets why they entered the work. This section is your recalibration. Use it when:

- disappointment, cynicism, or moral injury begins to creep in
- you feel you have lost your "why"
- you are carrying regret, anger, or accumulated emotional residue
- you want to lead ethically, not just win strategically

This is where you reconnect with justice as a human value, not merely a technical outcome. You remember that success without integrity is hollow, and that your legacy is shaped not only by what you achieve, but by **how you treat people while achieving it.**

**A Legal Practice, Not a Linear Path**

You may read in sequence, **Self → Practice → Purpose**, and allow the book to build you, layer by layer. Or you may open it like a professional tool: **go straight to what your current matter, season, or stress requires.** There is no "right pace" and no finish line. Some chapters will feel like confirmation. Others will feel like confrontation. Both are part of becoming unbound. Read slowly. Apply one practice. Return again. **Insight becomes transformation only when practised.**

**Your Commitment**

This book asks only one thing of you: **show up honestly.** Not as the flawless professional. Not as the performer. Not as the one who must always have the answer. Show up as the lawyer who is willing to be awake, willing to refine not only your skill, but your self, because the profession does not need more lawyers who are merely competent. It needs lawyers who are **clear, grounded, courageous, and humane.** Practise with precision. Lead with conscience. Serve justice, and remain unbound.

# INTRODUCTION

I am a practising lawyer. I have worked in private practice, in government, in education, and in defence. I am also an Associate Professor of Law. I know the discipline the profession demands, the precision, the accountability, the ethical responsibility, and the cumulative human consequence that legal work carries over time. This book was not written from outside the profession, nor from theory alone. It was written from within the work, from practice, teaching, reflection, and years of observing how law shapes not only outcomes, but the people entrusted to deliver them. Across every setting in which I have worked, the pattern is consistent. Lawyers are intelligent, committed, and capable. They are also under sustained pressure. They hold conflict, urgency, risk, and responsibility, often without space to process the personal cost of doing so. The profession trains us well in what to think, but far less in how to remain grounded, ethical, and whole while thinking and behaving under pressure. Most lawyers do not struggle because they lack competence. They struggle because competence is asked to carry everything. This book begins there.

## THE PROFESSION BETWEEN RIGOUR AND HUMANITY

Law must be rigorous. It must be exacting. The standards matter, and they should, but rigour alone does not sustain judgment. It does not protect conscience. It does not ensure longevity in practice. Over time, many lawyers develop habits that serve performance but quietly narrow inner capacity: emotional distance mistaken for professionalism, self-suppression framed as resilience, constant vigilance treated as normal. These patterns are understandable. They are often rewarded., but they are not neutral. Unchecked, they shape the lawyer in ways that reduce clarity, erode meaning, and increase burnout, not through failure, but through prolonged success without integration. **The Unbound Lawyer** does not argue for less discipline. It argues for deeper alignment.

## WHY THIS BOOK TAKES A DIFFERENT POSITION

This book sits at the intersection of **practice, education, and lived experience**. As a practising lawyer, I know what it is to make decisions under pressure, to advise where consequences are real, and to carry responsibility beyond the page. As an academic, I know how law is taught, assessed, and internalised, and how early habits of over-identification, perfectionism, and emotional suppression are often formed. Across both, I have seen what sustains good lawyers, and what quietly erodes them. The position of this book is simple and defensible:

- self-awareness is a professional skill
- emotional regulation is ethical infrastructure
- reflection is not retreat, but responsibility
- compassion and kindness strengthen judgment rather than weaken it

This is not wellbeing rhetoric. It is professional sustainability.

## THE STRUCTURE THAT FOLLOWS

The Unbound Lawyer unfolds through three disciplined movements:

- the lawyer as a person who must remain steady
- the lawyer in practice, exercising judgment and influence
- the lawyer over time, carrying purpose, consequence, and legacy

Each movement is grounded in recognised professional frameworks and designed to be applied, not admired. This is a book to return to, in moments of pressure, transition, doubt, or recalibration.

## A WORD TO YOU AS A PEER

If you are reading this, you are likely committed to the law. You may also recognise the quiet cost of carrying it well. This book does not ask you to step away from the profession. It asks you to practise with greater clarity, conscience, and care, without sacrificing rigour or authority. It is written peer-to-peer. Lawyer to lawyer. Teacher to practitioner. From within the profession, for those who intend to stay in it, and stay whole. Welcome to **The Unbound Lawyer**. A way of practising law that is exacting, humane, and sustainable, across a lifetime.

Time To Transform

EMPOWERING LIVES

# PART 1 - THE LAWYER BEHIND THE ROLE

### (Time to Transform: Living Unbound - Chapters 1 Breathing • 3 I Am… • 5 Mirror • 11 Grounding)

Before a lawyer can exercise sound judgment, the lawyer must be steady. Law is not practised in neutral conditions. It is practised under pressure, time pressure, emotional pressure, adversarial pressure, and moral pressure. Decisions are made with incomplete information, high consequence, and little margin for error. In these conditions, technical knowledge alone is not enough. Judgment depends on the internal state of the practitioner. This section exists for that reason. The four Modules in this opening movement, **Breathing, I Am…, Mirror, and Grounding**, were chosen because they address the *inner conditions that precede good lawyering.* They do not teach skills in the conventional sense. They restore capacity: the capacity to remain clear, regulated, and ethically anchored when the work is demanding. This is where the work begins, not because it is soft, but because it is structural.

### Why These Modules Matter in Legal Practice

**Breathing** is the most overlooked professional skill in law. Under sustained pressure, the nervous system narrows attention, accelerates reaction, and reduces cognitive flexibility. Lawyers may continue to function, but judgment becomes reactive rather than discerning. Breathing practices restore physiological regulation, allowing thinking to widen again. This module is not about relaxation for its own sake; it is about restoring the conditions for precise reasoning, measured response, and ethical restraint.

**I Am…** addresses identity, and identity is central to how lawyers experience pressure. Many lawyers unconsciously fuse their worth with performance, outcomes, or approval. When identity becomes over-attached to role, every matter feels personal, every loss feels like failure, and every mistake threatens self-concept. This module separates *who you are* from *what you do*, allowing you to practise with commitment without becoming consumed by outcome. For lawyers, this distinction is essential for longevity and integrity.

**Mirror** is the discipline of self-honesty. Legal training sharpens the ability to analyse others. It does not always cultivate the habit of examining oneself with the same rigour. This module invites structured reflection on bias, projection, emotional reaction, and ethical discomfort, not as self-criticism, but as professional calibration. The capacity to see oneself clearly is foundational to ethical decision-making and responsible use of authority.

**Grounding** restores stability in environments that reward constant vigilance. Lawyers often operate in heightened states of alert for extended periods. Over time, this becomes normalised, and damaging. Grounding practices return attention to the present moment, the body, and what is actually required now. This steadiness is not passive; it is what allows lawyers to remain composed in court, focused in negotiation, and measured in conflict. Together, these four modules create a **professional inner stance**: regulated, reflective, and anchored.

### When to Return to This Section

This section is designed to be returned to repeatedly throughout a legal career. It is particularly relevant when you are navigating:

- high-stakes matters with compressed timeframes
- courtroom nerves, performance pressure, or imposter thoughts
- conflict fatigue, vicarious trauma, or emotional overload
- perfectionism, people-pleasing, or the need to control outcomes
- ethical discomfort, frustration, or a sense of misalignment

These experiences are not signs of weakness. They are indicators that the internal load of practice is increasing. This section restores the internal authority that makes external authority trustworthy.

### The Deeper Purpose of Section One

In law, authority is often conferred by role, seniority, or title., but **true authority is sustained internally**. It arises when a lawyer can remain calm without detachment, confident without defensiveness, and decisive without aggression. Section One exists to rebuild that authority from the inside out.

It ensures that when you draft, advise, negotiate, or appear, you do so from steadiness rather than strain, from clarity rather than reactivity. This is not about becoming less engaged in the work. It is about becoming *less destabilised* by it. Only when the lawyer is grounded can the law be practised well.

# MODULE 1 – BREATHING

## Your Opening Reflection

**An Invitation to Breathe -** Before you move forward, allow yourself this simple gift: pause, soften, and breathe. Your breath is not just air, it is life moving through you, a gentle reminder that you are here, alive, and connected. Let each inhale welcome you home to your heart, and let each exhale release what no longer serves you. With every breath, you are reminded that presence, peace, and renewal are always within reach.

- "What does your breath feel like in this moment, tight, shallow, soft, steady?"
- "When you pause to breathe deeply, what changes within you, even slightly?"
- "What single word or phrase describes your relationship with your breath today?"
- "How does your body respond when you bring awareness to your heart as you breathe?"
- "What would it feel like to let your breath be your guide, instead of your mind?"

Let these questions open the doorway into presence. Every answer you give, whether in words, sensations, or silence, is a bridge between where you are and where you are going.

## Learning Objectives

The learning objectives are included here to give you a clear focus for this module, ensuring that each practice you explore moves you closer to mastering the skills, insights, and heart-led awareness that will enrich your life well beyond the program. By the end of this module, you will:

- Understand the role of breath in emotional regulation and self-awareness.
- Practice deep, heart-centred breathing techniques.
- Identify physical and emotional shifts that result from conscious breathwork.
- Connect with your heart space to access intuitive and emotional guidance.
- Develop a sustainable self-regulation practice anchored in conscious breathing.

**Core Emotional Domains**

The core emotional intelligence domains covered here are essential because they form the foundation for lasting heart connection, guiding you to deepen self-awareness, regulate emotions, build resilience, and strengthen the mind-body bond throughout your *Unbound* journey.

- **Self-Awareness:** Breath draws your attention inward, helping you notice your thoughts, feelings, and physical state.
- **Self-Regulation:** Conscious breathing soothes the nervous system and helps you respond rather than react.
- **Emotional Healing and Resilience:** Breath anchors you through emotional waves, creating space for release, reflection, and recovery.
- **Mind-Body Connection:** Breathing links your physical body with emotional presence, grounding you in calm awareness.

**"Breathing – The Bridge Between Your Mind, Body And Heart"**

<u>The Science and Soul of Breathing</u>

Breath is a bridge between your mind, body, and heart. Ancient traditions and neuroscience agree: breath regulates the nervous system, releases stress, and activates inner peace. Ancient traditions and modern neuroscience come together to affirm a timeless and powerful truth: your breath is one of the most effective regulators of your nervous system. Across thousands of years, wisdom traditions such as yoga, meditation, tai chi, and pranayama have harnessed the breath to still the mind, release stored tension, and open the doorway to inner peace. In these traditions, breath has never been only a biological function, it has been a sacred bridge between your body, your mind, and your spirit. Today, the precision of neuroscience confirms what those ancient practices have always known. Conscious breathing, especially slow, deep, and rhythmic breathing, activates your parasympathetic nervous system, signaling safety and calm to every cell in your body. It reduces the production of cortisol, the primary stress hormone, and restores balance in moments when life feels overwhelming. It creates a physiological shift away from the hyper-vigilance of fight-or-flight and into the grounded steadiness of rest-and-digest.

When you choose to slow down and breathe with intention, you are giving your body a clear message: *It is safe to let go.* This simple act changes your chemistry, softens the constant activity of your mind, and allows your awareness to expand. You step out of survival mode and into a deeper state of presence, one where you can think clearly, feel deeply, and respond rather than react. In this space, peace stops being a fleeting visitor and begins to feel like your natural state of being. Your breath is both an ancient ally and a scientifically validated tool, always within reach, waiting to guide you back to balance, clarity, and connection. It is the one practice that unites the wisdom of the past with the breakthroughs of the present, a living bridge between who you are now and the grounded, heart-led life you are capable of living.

**Conscious Breathing Helps Detoxify The Body, Increase Energy, Support Digestion, And Calm Emotional Responses**

When you breathe deeply and with full awareness, you awaken and activate your body's natural systems for healing, balance, and restoration. Each slow, intentional breath draws more oxygen into your lungs, delivering fresh life to your cells. This increase in oxygen flow helps to flush out toxins, revitalise your tissues, and renew your energy from the inside out. As you consciously breathe, you gently stimulate your parasympathetic nervous system, your body's "*rest and digest*" mode. This shifts you away from stress-driven states and into calm, steady balance. Your digestion improves, nutrient absorption is enhanced, and your entire internal system begins to function with greater ease and harmony. On an emotional level, each conscious breath is a reset button. It calms heightened stress responses, softens anxious thoughts, and clears mental fog. You create space between what you feel and how you respond, giving yourself the power to choose presence over reactivity. In this grounded state, you move from reacting impulsively to responding with clarity and intention. Your breath becomes more than an automatic process, it becomes your anchor, a reliable and profound tool that can realign your body, settle your mind, and harmonise your emotions in any moment you choose. It is always with you, ready to guide you back to balance whenever you need it most.

**The Role Of The Vagus Nerve In Emotional Regulation**

Your vagus nerve is one of the most vital yet often overlooked components of your emotional wellbeing. As the longest cranial nerve in your body, it acts as a major communication highway between your brain and vital organs, especially the heart, lungs, and digestive system, but beyond its physical functions, your vagus nerve plays a central role in your capacity to regulate emotions, connect with others, and return to calm after stress.

1. Your Built-In Reset Button

When you are overwhelmed or anxious, your sympathetic nervous system kicks in, this is the "*fight, flight, or freeze*" response. The vagus nerve is the primary activator of your parasympathetic nervous system, your body's "*rest and digest*" or "*tend and befriend*" mode. When stimulated, it sends signals that slow your heart rate, lower your blood pressure, deepen your breath, and signal safety to your brain. In essence, it tells your entire system: *It is okay. You are safe now.*

2. Your Vagus Nerve and the Emotion-Body Connection

Your emotions are not just "*in your head*", they are experienced throughout your body. The vagus nerve helps regulate this experience by transmitting information from the gut and heart to the brain and vice versa. This bidirectional communication helps shape how you feel and how quickly you recover from emotional upsets. A well-toned vagus nerve supports quicker emotional recovery, greater resilience, and an increased ability to stay grounded during stress.

3. Vagal Tone and Resilience

Vagal tone refers to how efficiently your vagus nerve performs. High vagal tone is associated with emotional flexibility, stronger relationships, better heart rate variability (HRV), and increased capacity for compassion and empathy. It means you can shift more easily from stress back to calm, think clearly under pressure, and respond instead of react. Low vagal tone, on the other hand, is often linked to anxiety, depression, digestive issues, and emotional dysregulation.

4. Practices That Activate your Vagus Nerve

You can tone and strengthen your vagus nerve with intentional daily practices:

- Deep diaphragmatic breathing (especially with longer exhales)
- Humming, chanting, or singing (activates the vocal cords connected to the vagus nerve)
- Cold exposure (e.g., splashing your face with cold water)
- Gentle yoga, grounding, or tai chi
- Loving-kindness meditation and connection with safe people
- Mindful touch or placing your hand on your heart

These practices are simple yet powerful ways to train your body to return to emotional balance more quickly and naturally.

5. Your Vagus Nerve and Heart Intelligence

Your vagus nerve also plays a critical role in what some call "*heart-brain coherence.*" When your breath, emotions, and nervous system are regulated, your heart rhythm becomes smooth and coherent. This coherence sends signals to your brain that create calm, clear thinking, and prosocial emotions such as gratitude, compassion, and love. It is through this heart-vagus-brain connection that you experience emotional intelligence at its most embodied level. In essence, your vagus nerve is a bridge between your body and your emotions, between survival and thriving. Learning to activate and care for this vital nerve is not just a wellness trend, it is a deep act of self-connection. When you tune into your vagus nerve, you reclaim your power to self-soothe, relate, and live from a grounded and open heart.

**The Difference Between Shallow And Deep Breathing**

Breathing is the most constant and essential act of your life, but not all breaths are created equal. How you breathe can profoundly affect your nervous system, emotional state, energy levels, and overall wellbeing. Understanding the difference between shallow and deep breathing gives you the power to regulate stress, improve focus, and connect more deeply with your body and heart.

Shallow Breathing: The Breath of Stress and Survival

Shallow breathing, also known as chest or thoracic breathing, is when you take quick, short breaths that primarily fill only the upper part of your lungs. It often goes unnoticed, yet it is common in daily life, especially when you are under pressure, anxious, or distracted.

Effects of Shallow Breathing:

- Activates your sympathetic nervous system (fight, flight, or freeze)
- Increases your heart rate and blood pressure
- Reduces oxygen exchange, which can cause fatigue, fogginess, or dizziness
- Restricts your diaphragm, your body's natural breathing muscle
- Can create a feedback loop of anxiety, where poor breathing fuels more tension

You might not even realise you are breathing shallowly, it has become a norm in high-stress, fast-paced environments. Over time, habitual shallow breathing can contribute to chronic stress, emotional imbalance, and disconnection from your body.

Deep Breathing: The Breath of Presence and Calm

Deep breathing, sometimes called diaphragmatic or belly breathing, involves drawing air deep into the lungs so the diaphragm expands downward, allowing your belly to rise gently. This type of breath is slower, fuller, and more nourishing, both physiologically and emotionally.

Benefits of Deep Breathing:

- Activates your parasympathetic nervous system (rest and digest)
- Lowers your cortisol and stress levels
- Improves oxygen flow, energy, and cellular health
- Calms your mind and relaxes your body
- Enhances heart-brain coherence and emotional regulation

Deep breathing is a direct and accessible way to ground yourself in the present moment. It creates space between stimulus and response, allowing you to feel more centred and make wiser choices.

Breath as a Bridge Between Mind and Body

Your breath is one of the few functions in your body that is both automatic and under your conscious control. This makes it a powerful tool for regulating your nervous system, mood, and mental state. Shallow breathing often reflects a state of unconscious reactivity, while deep breathing invites mindful awareness and heart connection.

Try This: Shift from Shallow to Deep

1. Place one hand on your chest and one on your belly.
2. Notice which one rises when you breathe.
3. Now, slow down your inhale and gently breathe into your belly.
4. Let your exhale be just a little longer than your inhale.
5. Repeat for a few minutes, staying present with each breath.

Summary

Shallow breathing is a signal of survival. Deep breathing is a practice of self-awareness and presence. When you choose to breathe deeply, you return to your body, regulate your emotions, and cultivate calm from the inside out. It is not just a technique, it is a form of self-kindness and emotional intelligence.

**Why Breath Awareness Equals Emotional Awareness**

Your breath is more than just a physiological process, it is an intimate reflection of your emotional state. Every emotion you feel subtly changes the rhythm, depth, and pace of your breath. In the same way, bringing conscious awareness to your breath becomes a powerful gateway into emotional awareness, regulation, and healing.

The Breath-Emotion Connection

When you feel anxious, your breath becomes short and rapid. When you are sad, it may be slow and heavy. Joy may bring a light, expansive breath. Anger can make your breathing sharp and fast. Even without thinking, your body responds to emotion through breath. This connection is not symbolic, it is neurological, hormonal, and physiological. Your breath and your emotions are intimately wired through the autonomic nervous system, particularly through the **vagus nerve**, which links your brain, heart, lungs, and gut. This means that by tuning into your breath, you are actually tuning into how your entire emotional system is operating in real time.

What Happens When You Pay Attention to Your Breath?

1. **You Notice Subtle Shifts:** Breath awareness brings you into the present moment, where you can begin to *feel* what is really happening inside,

sometimes before the mind can label it.

2. **You start noticing when you are tense**: When you are holding your breath, or when you are breathing too fast. These are cues that something emotional is arising.
3. **You Interrupt Autopilot Reactions**: Without awareness, emotions often run unconsciously, leading to impulsive reactions, but when you are aware of your breath, you create a pause. In that pause, you find choice. You find space. You begin to respond, not react.
4. **You Regulate Your Nervous System**: When you observe your breath and intentionally slow it down, you stimulate the **parasympathetic nervous system** (rest and digest), which helps regulate cortisol and reduce emotional overwhelm. This in turn makes you more resilient and clear-headed.

Breath as an Emotional Mirror

Think of your breath as a *mirror* for your emotional landscape:

- Shallow breath = fear or stress
- Uneven breath = anxiety or agitation
- Held breath = suppression or shock
- Deep, flowing breath = calm, grounded presence

Learning to read your breath is like learning a language your body has always spoken, but you may not have listened to.

From Awareness to Compassion

Breath awareness is not about control, it is about curiosity and compassion. It invites you to meet yourself where you are, without judgment. To notice your trembling breath in sadness. Your held breath in tension. The flutter in excitement, and by bringing love and presence to your breath, you offer love and presence to the emotion beneath it.

A Simple Practice: Breath Check-In

Take a moment, wherever you are. Close your eyes if you wish.

- Notice your breath.
- Is it deep or shallow? Fast or slow?
- What might your breath be telling you right now?

- Can you soften it… just a little?

Summary

Breath awareness is emotional awareness. Your breath is your body's emotional compass, always guiding you inward, offering insight, balance, and peace. When you listen to your breath, you are not just breathing, you are *feeling*, *understanding*, and *healing*. Breath is the language of your heart.

**Exercise: 3 Minute Detox & Reset Breath**

Purpose: To experience how conscious breathing supports detoxification, boosts your energy, aids digestion, and calms emotions.

1. Sit or stand comfortably. Close your eyes if you feel safe to do so.
2. Inhale deeply through your nose for a count of 4, feel your belly expand.
3. Hold the breath gently for 4 seconds - allow oxygen to circulate.
4. Exhale slowly through your mouth for a count of 6, release tension and toxins.
5. Repeat for 3 minutes, staying present with each breath.

Reflection Prompts:

1. How do you feel physically and emotionally after this practice?
2. Where might you be holding tension or resistance in your life?

**Case Study Discussion: Caitlyn's Journey**

Caitlyn once described herself as an anxious, restless, and highly energetic woman, always in motion yet feeling strangely absent from her own life. For as long as she could remember, she had felt disconnected from her body, a separation born from the emotional wounds and traumas she had endured over the years. She never felt truly safe expressing her feelings or emotions, and so, without even realising it, she had built walls around her inner world, cutting herself off from her own heart as a means of self-protection. When we began practising balanced heart breathing, Caitlyn admitted that the process felt both strange and deeply uncomfortable. It was confrontational, not because the technique was difficult, but because for the first time in decades she was allowing herself to pause, to be fully present, and to listen to the quiet truth of her heart. The stillness brought her face-to-face with emotions she had long buried.

We often returned to the old saying, "*What you resist will persist.*" The more she resisted facing these emotions, the more they silently shaped her life. Yet, with each deep, conscious breath, Caitlyn began to shift. She found moments of peace she had not known in years. She felt balanced, grounded, and connected to herself in a way that was entirely new. The practice unlocked suppressed feelings, but instead of being overwhelmed, she began to meet them with compassion. Over time, the balanced heart breathing became her anchor. She opened up in ways she never imagined possible, and in doing so, she began to heal, to learn, and to grow. She found forgiveness, for herself, and for others, and she discovered a deep well of self-love she had never touched before. Today, Caitlyn's transformation is profound. She now teaches deep breathwork as part of her yoga practice, guiding others to find the same peace, connection, and inner freedom that reshaped her life. Her journey is living proof that the simple act of breathing with awareness can open the door to a life of balance, wholeness, and love.

**Reflective Exercise: Caitlyn's Journey**

Here are four profound and reflective questions inspired by Caitlyn's story:

1. In what ways might you be unconsciously disconnecting from your own emotions or body as a form of protection?
2. How do you typically respond when asked to slow down and be fully present, do you resist it, avoid it, or embrace it?
3. What emotions or memories arise when you begin to breathe deeply and consciously? How do you usually respond to them?
4. What would it mean for you to create a safe space, within yourself, to feel, release, and heal long-held emotions?

### Heart Whisper Affirmations For Integration

Affirmations have the power to quiet the noise of doubt, open the doorway to self-trust, and draw you back into the wisdom of your heart. When practised daily, they nurture an inner dialogue based in love and truth, helping you live each day more aligned with who you truly are. I invite you to repeat silently or write:

- *I feel centred and calm when I focus on my breath.*
- *I am able to quiet my mind through deep breathing.*

- *Breathing deeply helps me to release tension in my body.*
- *I find peace in the rhythm of my breath.*
- *My breath is a reminder to stay present in the moment.*
- *Through conscious breathing, I nurture inner harmony.*
- *Each breath I take fills me with clarity and light.*
- *With every exhale, I release what no longer serves me.*
- *My breath connects me to my heart and to the present moment.*
- *Breathing with awareness helps me move through life with ease and grace.*
- *My breath is my constant companion, guiding me back to peace.*

**Application Exercise: In-the-Moment Breathing Anchor**

**Purpose:** To centre yourself, regulate your nervous system, and reconnect with your heart's wisdom during moments of stress, anxiety, or emotional overload.

**Step-by-Step Practice:**

**1. Pause and Become Aware:** Gently stop what you are doing, and acknowledge what you are feeling without judgment. Name it if you can: *"I feel anxious, overwhelmed, tense…"*

**2. Place Your Hand on Your Heart**: This simple gesture activates oxytocin (the calming hormone) and helps your body feel safe. Feel the warmth and weight of your hand. Let it be an anchor to the present moment.

**3. Begin Balanced Heart Breathing (3 Rounds)**: Inhale slowly through your nose for **4 seconds.** Exhale gently through your mouth for **6 seconds.** Repeat **3 times**, focusing on softening your shoulders and relaxing your jaw

**4. Ask Your Heart:**: *"What do I need in this moment?"* Be still and listen, your heart may answer with a word, a feeling, or a sense of direction (e.g., *rest, space, support, courage, nothing at all*) Trust whatever comes up, even if it is silence.

**Close with Compassion**

Affirm: *"I honour how I feel, and I give myself what I need."* Gently return to your day with renewed presence.

**Closing Reflection**

Breath is more than survival, it is a sacred rhythm, a quiet guide, and a constant companion. Today, you have taken your first step into reconnecting with your breath not just as a function, but as a bridge to your heart. With each conscious inhale and exhale, you create space for clarity, healing, and grounded presence. In slowing down, you have begun to listen, not just to your breath, but to the quiet wisdom within you. This is more than a practice; it is a return. A return to yourself. Trust that your breath will meet you in every moment, and guide you gently, truthfully, toward peace and emotional wholeness.

**The Path Opens Further**

You have taken a step. The next step is waiting. Every book in the Unbound Series widens the path, deeper into your story, sharper into your strengths, and closer to the life you were meant to live.When you are ready, turn the page into the next Unbound journey – www.timetotransform.world

# MODULE 2 – I AM

## Your Opening Reflection

An Invitation to Enter the Doorway of Presence - Before you move further, I invite you to pause. Let the pace of the world fall away for a moment. Breathe gently. Place your hand over your heart if it feels right, and allow yourself to arrive fully here. These questions are not meant to be solved with your mind, but to be received with your heart. Let them open you, soften you, and guide you into deeper presence. However your heart responds, with words, feelings, or simple stillness, is enough. This is your doorway. Step through gently, and let your truth meet you here.

- "What truth within you is ready to be seen and embraced?"
- "How can you honour the most authentic part of yourself right now?"
- "Where is your heart inviting you to soften, open, or trust more deeply?"
- "Who are you in this moment?"
- "What does your heart long for you to know today?"

Let these questions open the doorway into presence. Every answer you give, whether in words, sensations, or silence, is a bridge between where you are and where you are going.

## Learning Objectives

The learning objectives are included here to give you a clear focus for this module, ensuring that each practice you explore moves you closer to mastering the skills, insights, and heart-led awareness that will enrich your life well beyond the program. By the end of this module, you will:

- Understand the emotional and psychological significance of *'I am'* statements.
- Apply self-affirmation techniques to develop self-awareness, self-love, and resilience.
- Identify and challenge your negative self-talk and limiting beliefs.
- Integrate heart-led *'I am'* practices into your daily emotional regulation strategies.
- Reflect on your core identity and values through the lens of emotional intelligence.

**Core Emotional Domains**

The core emotional intelligence domains covered here are essential because they form the foundation for lasting heart connection, guiding you to deepen self-awareness, regulate emotions, build resilience, and strengthen the mind-body bond throughout your Unbound journey.

- **Self-awareness** – You deepen your ability to notice and name your inner experiences with honesty and clarity.
- **Self-regulation** – You learn to respond with calm and choice, rather than react with impulse or overwhelm.
- **Motivation** – You connect with your heart's purpose, cultivating inner drive grounded in meaning and intention.
- **Empathy (Self-Compassion)** – You develop kindness toward yourself, embracing your humanity with gentleness and care.
- **Social Skills (through shared reflections and storytelling)** – You build authentic connection by listening deeply, sharing truthfully, and growing together.

**"I Am – Affirming Your Self Worth"**

The words "*I Am*" hold profound historical, spiritual, and psychological power. Across traditions and philosophies, they have been used as declarations of identity, intention, and transformation. In ancient spiritual texts, such as the Hebrew Bible, "*I Am*" was spoken as a sacred name of the divine, pointing to the infinite, unchanging essence of being. Similarly, in Eastern traditions, the phrase reflects the awareness of consciousness itself, pure presence without attachment to roles or labels. Psychologically, "*I am*" statements shape the core of your self-identity. When you repeat phrases like "*I am strong*," "*I am not enough*," or "*I am unworthy*," you are not just describing how you feel, you are shaping how you see yourself. These internal narratives form the foundation of your self-image, influencing how you show up in relationships, how you handle adversity, and how you pursue your goals. By consciously choosing "*I am*" statements that reflect truth, possibility, and self-compassion, you rewire your emotional pathways. You begin to let go of inherited beliefs or imposed identities that no longer serve you. When you say, "*I am whole*," or "*I am becoming*," you begin to step into a more aligned version of yourself, one based in presence, resilience, and self-awareness. In *The Unbound Leader* program, "*I am*" becomes more than a statement. It becomes a practice. A powerful reminder that you are not defined by your past, your mistakes, or your fears. You are a living expression of growth, capable of healing, belonging, and becoming.

<u>Ancient traditions and spiritual roots of '*I am*' – Egypt</u>

In ancient Egyptian spirituality, the phrase "*I Am*" was deeply intertwined with divine identity, sacred knowledge, and cosmic truth. The Egyptians believed in the power of spoken words, particularly in connection with the soul (ba), essence (ka), and the divine self. To say "*I Am*" was to affirm one's alignment with the eternal, the divine order (ma'at), and the living gods who dwelled within and beyond.

**Examples:**

1. **The Book of the Dead** – The deceased declares "*I Am*" statements like "*I am Atum*," "*I am yesterday, today, and tomorrow*," to affirm oneness with the gods and pass safely into the afterlife.
2. **Pharaoh's Declarations** – Pharaohs, seen as divine rulers, used "*I Am*" statements to assert their identity as living gods on earth (e.g., "*I am Horus, the falcon of the horizon*").
3. **Temple Inscriptions** – Priestly texts included affirmations like "*I Am the flame that shineth*," symbolising divine presence and eternal life within the human soul.

These affirmations were tools of empowerment and alignment with divine truth.

<u>Ancient traditions and spiritual roots of '*I am*' – Christianity</u>

In Christianity, the phrase "*I Am*" carries profound theological and spiritual significance. It originates in the Old Testament when God reveals His name to Moses as "*I AM WHO I AM*" (Exodus 3:14), signifying eternal presence, self-existence, and divine authority. In the New Testament, Jesus uses "*I Am*" statements to affirm his divine nature and connection with God, offering powerful metaphors for spiritual identity, truth, and transformation.

**Examples:**

1. **Exodus 3:14** – God tells Moses, "*I AM WHO I AM,*" establishing the sacred, unchanging identity of the Divine.
2. **John 8:58** – Jesus declares, "*Before Abraham was, I Am,*" aligning himself directly with the eternal nature of God.
3. **John 14:6** – "*I Am the way, the truth, and the life*" – Jesus reveals the path to spiritual fulfillment and connection with God through identity and faith.

In Christianity, "*I Am*" is both a declaration of divine presence and an invitation to discover your own identity in relationship with God.

Ancient traditions and spiritual roots of '*I am*' – Islam

In Islam, while the direct phrase "*I Am*" is used less explicitly than in other traditions, its spiritual essence is deeply embedded in the Qur'an and Sufi teachings. The Divine Names of Allah (Asma'ul Husna) reflect aspects of being and identity, and believers are encouraged to reflect these attributes through their own character. The Islamic understanding of self (nafs) involves a journey of purification, moving closer to God (Allah) by aligning one's inner being with divine will. In this sense, "*I Am*" becomes a reflection of one's spiritual striving, based in humility and remembrance (dhikr).

**Examples:**

1. **Qur'an 20:14** – Allah says, *"Indeed, I am Allah. There is no deity except Me, so worship Me and establish prayer for My remembrance."* This is a divine assertion of eternal being and presence.
2. **Sufi Mysticism** – Poets like Rumi and Al-Hallaj speak of divine union using language that reflects a purified self, where "*I am*" becomes a vessel for divine love and oneness. Al-Hallaj famously said, *"Ana al-Haqq" (I am the Truth),* expressing mystical unity with the Divine.

3. **99 Names of Allah** – Believers may reflect on names such as *Al-Rahman* (The Compassionate) and say, "*I am striving to be compassionate*," as a way of embodying divine qualities in human form.

In Islam, "*I Am*" is a journey toward divine remembrance, grounded in surrender, humility, and alignment with God's attributes.

Ancient traditions and spiritual roots of '*I Am*' – Judaism

In Judaism, gratitude is a core spiritual practice that shapes your daily life and relationship with God. You are encouraged to begin each day with *Modeh Ani*, a prayer of thanks for the gift of life. Gratitude is seen not just as a feeling, but as a disciplined act of recognition for God's constant presence, mercy, and provision. Through blessings, prayers, and ethical action, you cultivate awareness that everything you receive is a reflection of divine grace and responsibility.

**Examples**

1. You recite blessings (*brachot*) throughout the day, to give thanks for food, nature, learning, and joyful experiences.
2. You observe Shabbat with a grateful heart, pausing to rest and reflect on the blessings of creation and community.
3. You express gratitude through *tzedakah* (charity), sharing your resources to help others as a sacred obligation grounded in thankfulness.

In Judaism, gratitude is more than a feeling, it is a way of being that shapes who you are. Through daily prayers, blessings, and acts of kindness, you affirm *I am grateful*, recognising that each moment, each gift, and each breath is part of a greater divine flow.

Ancient traditions and spiritual roots of '*I am*' – Buddhism

In Buddhism, the concept of "*I am*" is examined through the lens of impermanence and the illusion of a fixed self. Rather than affirming a permanent identity, Buddhist teachings invite you to observe and ultimately release attachment to the ego. The "*self*" is seen as a collection of changing processes, form, sensation, perception, mental formations, and consciousness (the five aggregates). True freedom comes not from asserting "*I am*," but from realising that clinging to this identity causes suffering. Still, deep spiritual insight can arise through compassionate awareness of your conditioned self.

**Examples:**

1. **The Anatta Doctrine (No-Self)** – The Buddha taught that there is no permanent, unchanging "*I*." Understanding this liberates you from suffering and ego attachment.
2. **The Heart Sutra** – "*Form is emptiness, emptiness is form.*" This reflects the view that what you perceive as "I am" is not solid, but a flow of experience and consciousness.
3. **Mindfulness Practice** – In meditation, you may notice thoughts like "*I am angry*" or "*I am not good enough*" and learn to see them as passing mental states, not truths. This creates space for compassion, clarity, and transformation.

In Buddhism, spiritual growth involves softening the grip of "*I am*" to find deeper freedom and peace.

<u>Ancient traditions and spiritual roots of '*I am*' – Hinduism</u>

In Hinduism, the phrase "*I am*" carries deep spiritual significance, often reflecting the sacred unity between the individual self (*atman*) and the universal consciousness (*Brahman*). Based in the Upanishads and Vedantic philosophy, the understanding of "*I am*" transcends the ego and points toward self-realisation, the awareness that your true essence is divine. Rather than being limited by name, form, or identity, "*I am*" becomes a powerful affirmation of spiritual truth and oneness with all life. The journey of the soul is to awaken from illusion (*maya*) and remember: "*I am That*" (*Aham Brahmasmi*).

**Examples:**

1. **Aham Brahmasmi** – Found in the Brihadaranyaka Upanishad, this means "*I am Brahman*," a profound realisation that your innermost self is not separate from the Divine.
2. **Bhagavad Gita (Chapter 10, Verse 20)** – Krishna says, *"I am the Self, O Gudakesha, seated in the hearts of all creatures."* This reveals that divinity resides within every being.
3. **Meditative Mantras** – Practices such as silently repeating "*So Hum*" ("*I am That*") during meditation help dissolve the ego and align your awareness with universal consciousness.

In Hinduism, "*I am*" is not just identity, it is a sacred doorway to self-realisation, inner peace, and divine unity.

## The Psychology Of Self-Affirmation And Neuroplasticity

Self-affirmation is more than positive thinking, it is a psychological process based in the deep human need to preserve integrity and identity, especially when faced with challenge or threat. By consciously affirming your core values, strengths, or beliefs, you reinforce a coherent sense of self, which helps buffer against stress, anxiety, and self-doubt. Psychologists have found that self-affirmation reduces defensiveness, enhances problem-solving, and increases emotional resilience. From a neuroscience perspective, self-affirmation activates regions of your brain associated with reward and self-processing, such as your ventromedial prefrontal cortex. Over time, with consistent practice, these affirmations begin to reshape neural patterns through a process called neuroplasticity, your brain's ability to change and adapt. When you repeat empowering statements like "*I am worthy*," "*I am enough*," or "*I am loved*," you strengthen new neural pathways that reinforce positive self-belief and emotional regulation. Ultimately, self-affirmation and neuroplasticity work together to support healing, growth, and transformation, empowering you to rewrite your internal narrative and live with greater authenticity, confidence, and connection.

<u>Self-Affirmation & Neuroplasticity: Key Insights</u>

- **Self-affirmation is a psychological process:** Helps preserve your identity and integrity, especially in moments of stress or challenge.
- **Affirming your core values strengthens your sense of self:** Reduces anxiety, self-doubt, and defensiveness.
- **Psychological benefits:** Enhances emotional resilience, clarity, and problem-solving ability.
- **Neuroscience perspective:** Activates brain regions linked to reward and self-processing (e.g., ventromedial prefrontal cortex).
- **Neuroplasticity in action:** Repeating affirmations like "*I am enough*" reshapes brain pathways, reinforcing self-belief and calm.
- **Empowerment through repetition:** Regular practice rewires your mindset, enabling personal transformation.
- **The outcome:** Greater confidence, emotional regulation, and alignment with your authentic self.

**Modern Thinkers & The Rise Of Positive Affirmations**

**Louise Hay:** A pioneer in self-healing and affirmations. Her bestselling book *You Can Heal Your Life* (1984) introduced millions to the idea that thoughts can shape reality. She taught that repeating positive *"I am"* statements could transform health, self-worth, and life circumstances. Her work helped bridge spirituality and psychology for a mainstream audience.

**Wayne Dyer:** Often called the *"father of motivation,"* Dyer merged psychology, spirituality, and self-empowerment. In books like *The Power of Intention* and *You will See It When You Believe It*, he taught that affirmations direct energy and shape outcomes. Dyer emphasised that *"I am"* statements align individuals with their divine nature and higher potential.

Their Legacy: Both thinkers helped move affirmations from fringe self-help to mainstream personal development. Their teachings continue to influence emotional intelligence, wellness programs, and even therapeutic practices today.

> **Reflection Prompt: *"Think about a time when your inner dialogue shaped your outlook or choices. What would have changed if, in that moment, you affirmed your worth or potential instead?"***
>
> Take a few moments to journal a positive "*I am*" statement that feels true or needed today (e.g., *I am healing, I am more than enough, I am safe to grow*). Reflect on how repeating this could gently reshape your beliefs, emotions, or actions over time.

**Emotional Resilience and Self-Love Through Daily 'I Am' Practices**

**Daily *'I am'* statements** are more than words, they are intentional declarations that shape your inner narrative and sense of identity. Each repetition rewires how you see yourself and respond to the world. **Emotional resilience** grows when you affirm truths like *"I am strong," "I am calm in the storm,"* or *"I am grounded."* These statements help regulate your nervous system, shift your mindset, and buffer against life's challenges. **Self-love deepens** as you consistently speak to yourself with kindness and encouragement. Affirmations dissolve layers of shame, self-doubt, and internalised criticism, replacing them with compassion and self-acceptance. From a **neuroscience perspective**, daily affirmations activate regions of your brain involved in self-perception and emotional regulation (e.g., the ventromedial prefrontal cortex). This promotes **neuroplasticity**, strengthening pathways that support healthy self-belief. Over time, your inner voice transforms from a critic to a **source of safety and strength**, guiding you back to your heart when you feel lost or overwhelmed. Practising *'I am'* affirmations daily is a **deliberate act of self-leadership**, empowering you to live in alignment with your truth, confident, connected, and compassionate.

**'*I am*' - Exercise**

**Hearting Exercise – Mirror Work & Voice Activation**

1. Stand or sit in front of a mirror.
2. Place your hand on your heart.
3. Say aloud five chosen '*I am*' statements (e.g. "*I am worthy of love,*" "*I am enough.*")
4. Observe the emotions that surface. Do not judge, just notice and breathe through them.

**Personal Reflection - Journalling Prompts:**

- *"Which 'I am' statement felt most empowering or most uncomfortable?"*
- *"Where do you still withhold love or affirmation from yourself, and why?"*
- *"How can you nurture that part of you more consciously?"*

**Case Study Discussion: Sophie's Journey**

I remember Sophie many years ago when she chose to start truly loving herself. It was a real battle, and she would be the first to admit that it took her a long time to be comfortable with saying ANYTHING positive about herself and who she was. Sophie had been in an emotionally abusive marriage that had taken a mental and an emotional toll on her and eroded her confidence, self–worth, and self–esteem. Sophies self–talk was highly destructive and restricted her ability to love herself and live her best life. When I started this hearting exercise with Sophie, she was unable to say or write anything positive, loving, caring, or nurturing about herself. Over the course of six months, we journeyed together and brought her to a place where she could face herself in the mirror, put her hand on her heart and say, '*I am worthy of love.*' That was a beautiful day indeed! Your journey to self is about KNOWING who you are. You may think that you already know who you are, but do you truly FEEL it at your core and in your heart? How do you talk to yourself?

**Reflective Exercise – Sophie's Story**

Here are five profound and reflective questions inspired by Sophie's story:

1. **What are the words that follow your "*I am*"?:** *You shape your identity with every "I am" you speak. Are your words uplifting or limiting?*
2. **When did you first learn to doubt your worth?** *Reflect on a moment when you stopped believing you were enough, and how that belief shaped you.*
3. **How does your body respond when you say something kind to yourself?** *Notice the physical and emotional impact of self-affirmation, your heart knows the truth.*
4. **What would change in your life if you truly believed "I am worthy of love"?** *Explore how a single belief could shift your relationships, decisions, and self-perception.*
5. **What truth does your heart long for you to claim with your "I am"?** *Give voice to the part of you that's been waiting to be seen, honoured, and embraced.*

These questions help you recognise how "*I am*" statements become a bridge between self-awareness and self-love.

**Affirmations For Integration (Heart Whispers)**

Affirmations have the power to quiet the noise of doubt, open the doorway to self-trust, and draw you back into the wisdom of your heart. When practised daily, they nurture an inner dialogue based in love and truth, helping you live each day more aligned with who you truly are. I invite you to repeat silently or write:

- *I am worthy of love and respect.*
- *I am empowered to achieve my goals.*
- *I am responsible for my own happiness.*
- *I am grateful for what I have.*
- *I am open to new opportunities and experiences.*
- *I am constantly learning and growing*

- *I am aligned with the truth of my heart.*
- *I am deserving of peace, joy, and fulfilment.*
- *I am strong enough to face and overcome challenges.*
- *I am a source of love and kindness in the world.*

**Application Exercise - Begin Your Personal Affirmation Series**

Affirmations are not just words; they are seeds you plant in the garden of your mind. When repeated with intention, they can rewire the way you think, speak, and show up in the world. This 7-day challenge is an invitation to consciously shape your inner dialogue so it reflects the person you are becoming.

1. **Write Five *'I Am'* Statements:** Choose statements that feel truthful but also aspirational, bridging who you are now with who you are growing into. Example:
    - I am grounded and calm, no matter what comes my way.
    - I am worthy of love and respect.
    - I am a creative force, bringing value to the world.

Write them in the present tense as though they are already true.

2. **Place Them Where You Will See Them Often:** Write each statement on a sticky note or small card and put them in places where your eyes will land frequently, your bathroom mirror, your desk, your fridge, the inside of your journal, your phone's home screen. These small visual reminders keep your affirmations alive throughout the day.
3. **Speak Them Out Loud Daily:** Every morning and evening, stand tall, take a deep breath, and say each affirmation out loud. Look into your own eyes if you are in front of a mirror. Speak with conviction, as though you are telling yourself the most important truth you have ever known.
4. **Track Your Energy and Self-Talk:** Over the next 7 days, notice shifts, subtle or significant, in how you speak to yourself, how you react to challenges, and how you carry yourself. You may find your inner critic softening, your confidence growing, or your mood lifting.

**Reflection Prompt at the End of the Week:**

- Which affirmation felt most powerful for you, and why?
- Where did you notice the biggest shift in your thoughts, feelings, or behaviours?

**Closing Reflection**

You have journeyed into the sacred terrain of your own identity, the quiet, powerful space where the words *"I am"* shape your reality, your worth, and your path forward. Inqa a world that often tries to define you, declaring *"I am"* from the depth of your own heart is a courageous act of truth. It is not about ego or performance, it is about returning to your essence, remembering who you have always been beneath the noise, the pain, and the expectations. Each time you say *"I am worthy," "I am enough,"* or *"I am love,"* you reclaim your power. You begin to rewrite old narratives, gently rewire your inner world, and step more fully into who you truly are, not because something was broken, but because you are finally seeing your light clearly. Let this be your daily rhythm: not asking the world who you are, but remembering that you already know. You are the author of your "*I am*." Speak it with love. Live it with courage. Trust it with all your heart.

**The Path Opens Further**

You have taken a step. The next step is waiting. Every book in the Unbound Series widens the path, deeper into your story, sharper into your strengths, and closer to the life you were meant to live.When you are ready, turn the page into the next Unbound journey – www.timetotransform.world

# MODULE 3 – MIRROR

## Your Opening Reflection

**An Invitation to See Yourself with Gentle Eyes** - As you step into this module, I invite you to pause and soften. Take a breath, and allow yourself to meet the mirror not as an enemy, but as a friend. The reflection before you is not asking for perfection, only honesty, tenderness, and presence. Let this moment be an opening, a chance to see yourself not through judgment, but through love.

- "Are you willing to see the parts of yourself you usually hide?"
- "What truths about yourself are you ready to accept today?"
- "When you meet your own gaze, do you recognise your inherent worth?"
- "When you look in the mirror, what do you really see?"
- "Do you offer yourself love and kindness… or judgment?"

Let these questions open the doorway into presence. Every answer you give, whether in words, sensations, or silence, is a bridge between where you are and where you are going.

## Learning Objectives

The learning objectives are included here to give you a clear focus for this module, ensuring that each practice you explore moves you closer to mastering the skills, insights, and heart-led awareness that will enrich your life well beyond the program. By the end of this module, you will:

- Understand the emotional impact and science behind mirror work.
- Apply mirror work techniques to build yourself-worth, self-love, and emotional resilience.

- Identify internal resistance to self-acceptance and begin the process of transformation.
- Practice heart-connected affirmation and forgiveness through eye-gazing and mirror-based self-dialogue.
- Recognise how mirror work supports long-term emotional intelligence development and heart connection.

**Core Emotional Domains**

The core emotional intelligence domains covered here are essential because they form the foundation for lasting heart connection, guiding you to deepen self-awareness, regulate emotions, build resilience, and strengthen the mind-body bond throughout your *Unbound* journey.

- **Self-Awareness:** Helps you honestly see and acknowledge your emotions and inner dialogue as you face yourself.
- **Self-Regulation:** Enables you to stay grounded and calm when uncomfortable feelings surface during mirror work.
- **Motivation:** Fuels your commitment to personal growth and keeps you returning to the practice with intention.
- **Self-Compassion:** Encourages a kind, gentle response to your reflection, replacing criticism with understanding.
- **Emotional Resilience:** Strengthens your ability to move through vulnerability and transform emotional pain into healing.

**"Mirror - Facing Yourself With Love"**

<u>The Psychological, Emotional, and Spiritual Value of Mirror Work</u>

Mirror work is a courageous act of self-witnessing. It invites you to stand before your own reflection and meet the person who looks back, not with judgment, but with awareness, honesty, and compassion. This seemingly simple practice holds profound **psychological**, **emotional**, and **spiritual** value, especially when integrated into a heart-led path of healing and self-affirmation.

<u>Psychological Value</u>

From a psychological standpoint, mirror work is a powerful tool for increasing **self-awareness**. When you consciously look into your own eyes and speak to yourself with intention, you confront the often unconscious inner dialogue that runs beneath your surface thoughts. Over time, you begin to notice the beliefs you have inherited, the wounds you have carried, and the stories you have internalised about your worth. By practicing positive affirmations like "*I am enough*" or "*I am worthy of love,*" you start to **reprogram negative self-beliefs** and create new neural pathways through the science of **neuroplasticity**. This consistent, mindful reinforcement can shift your self-perception and support long-term cognitive and emotional growth.

<u>Emotional Value</u>

Emotionally, mirror work helps you build **emotional resilience**. It allows you to feel what you have suppressed, grief, shame, anger, joy, and to welcome those feelings without turning away. When you stand in front of the mirror and acknowledge your emotional truth, you begin to **regulate your emotional responses** with more clarity and compassion. This act of presence with your own emotional experience cultivates **self-acceptance** and nurtures a profound connection between your inner world and outer expression. Over time, this emotional honesty strengthens your capacity to hold space for others as well, enhancing empathy and relational depth.

<u>Spiritual Value</u>

Spiritually, mirror work becomes a sacred space, a daily ritual where you meet your soul. As you look into your own eyes, you begin to see not just your physical self, but the deeper essence that lives beneath your skin. This connection awakens your **inner wisdom**, your **divine light**, and the quiet voice of your heart. You begin to **recognise yourself as whole and loved**, regardless of past mistakes or external validation. In this space, the mirror becomes a metaphor for truth, reflecting not just who you are, but who you are becoming. It is a practice of **remembrance**, returning you to the truth that you are enough, just as you are. **In essence**, mirror work integrates psychological insight, emotional healing, and spiritual connection into a daily act of self-honouring. It helps you rewrite your internal narrative, build compassion from the inside out, and live with greater authenticity, presence, and love. When you dare to face yourself, gently, bravely, and consistently, you begin to unbind your heart and unlock the sacred power that lives within you.

### The Origin Of Mirror Work: Louise Hay's Legacy

Mirror work, as a transformative healing practice, finds its modern roots in the pioneering work of **Louise Hay,** an internationally renowned author, speaker, and the founder of Hay House Publishing. Often called the "*Queen of Affirmations*," Hay revolutionised the self-help landscape by introducing a profoundly simple yet emotionally powerful method: **mirror work,** the practice of looking into your own eyes in a mirror while speaking affirming, loving, and healing words to yourself. At the heart of Hay's philosophy was the belief that **self-love is the key to healing**. In her seminal book, *You Can Heal Your Life* (1984), she taught that most suffering, whether emotional, physical, or spiritual, stems from **negative self-beliefs, self-criticism, and unhealed emotional wounds**, often based in childhood. Mirror work, she believed, was a way to gently bring those wounds to the surface and meet them with compassion rather than judgment. The mirror became, in Hay's hands, a **sacred tool for self-confrontation and self-connection**. It bypassed the intellect and tapped directly into the heart. When you stand before a mirror and say, "*I love you*," or "*I am willing to change*," you are not just speaking words, you are rewiring beliefs, rewriting narratives, and restoring trust in yourself. Hay often said, *"The mirror reflects back to us the feelings we have about ourselves,"* and that reflection, when met with courage and consistency, becomes a gateway to healing.

The emotional impact of mirror work can be immediate and intense. Many people experience tears, resistance, even anger, as long-buried shame, fear, or grief rises to the surface. Yet with continued practice, mirror work becomes a daily ritual of **self-reclamation,** a way to rebuild inner safety, validate your worth, and awaken to your true nature. From a **psychological perspective**, mirror work helps interrupt cycles of negative self-talk, strengthens self-compassion, and promotes emotional regulation. From a **spiritual perspective**, it aligns you with the divine within, reminding you that you are inherently worthy, lovable, and whole. Hay's legacy lives on not just in her writings but in the countless lives transformed through her teachings. Her work paved the way for a generation of coaches, therapists, and spiritual leaders who continue to use mirror work as a foundation for emotional intelligence, trauma recovery, and self-love. To engage in mirror work is to return home to yourself. It is a commitment to **see, hear, and honour the person looking back at you,** not as broken, but as beautifully becoming. Through this practice, you are invited to dissolve the layers of fear, shame, and self-doubt and remember this fundamental truth: **your heart is the most powerful healer you have.**

## The Science Behind Mirror Work: Neuroplasticity, NLP, And Emotional Reprogramming

1. Neuroplasticity - Rewiring the Brain Through Repetition and Intention

At the core of mirror work lies the principle of **neuroplasticity,** your brain's innate ability to change and reorganise its neural pathways in response to thoughts, experiences, and behaviors. When you stand in front of a mirror and repeat empowering affirmations like "*I am enough*" or "*I am worthy of love,*" you are not just speaking words, you are sending new signals through your brain's emotional and cognitive circuits.

Repeated mirror affirmations:

- Activate regions such as the **ventromedial prefrontal cortex** (associated with self-referential thinking and emotional regulation).
- Begin to **overwrite old narratives** stored in your subconscious, often tied to shame, rejection, or inadequacy.
- **Strengthen neural connections** that align with self-worth, compassion, and inner peace.

This consistent rewiring process gradually **shifts your inner default** from self-criticism to self-acceptance. It creates a new emotional baseline where confidence and calm become more natural responses.

2. NLP - Anchoring and Reframing Limiting Beliefs

**Neuro-Linguistic Programming (NLP)** is a psychological approach that studies how language and behavior influence your brain. Mirror work draws from two powerful NLP techniques:

- **Anchoring**: By placing your hand over your heart, making eye contact with your reflection, and pairing these gestures with positive affirmations, you create an anchor, a physiological and emotional cue that triggers feelings of safety, warmth, and empowerment. Over time, just returning to the mirror with this gesture can evoke those same emotional states.
- **Reframing**: Many people carry internal scripts like "*I am not good enough,*" "*I do not matter,*" or "*I always fail.*" NLP teaches that by consciously **replacing these limiting beliefs** with affirmations such as "*I am growing,*" "*I am loved,*" or "*I am resilient,*" you shift your perception of self

and reality. Mirror work makes this reframe **visceral and immediate**, amplifying its effectiveness through direct self-confrontation.

3. Emotional Reprogramming - Healing Through Presence and Self-Compassion

Mirror work also accesses your **limbic system**, your brain's emotional centre. When you speak to yourself with sincerity, while making gentle eye contact, your nervous system receives the message that **you are safe, seen, and accepted**. This is emotionally powerful, especially for those who never received that validation from others. Emotional reprogramming through mirror work:

- Creates **new emotional memory patterns** that create trust and compassion.
- Reduces cortisol and supports parasympathetic nervous system activation, bringing **calm and regulation**.
- Encourages the release of **suppressed emotions** in a safe and self-directed environment.

Over time, the act of meeting yourself in the mirror with love helps you **dismantle shame**, **release stored trauma**, and **cultivate deep emotional resilience**.

Final Insight: A Whole-Person Transformation

When combined, neuroplasticity, NLP, and emotional reprogramming make mirror work a truly integrative healing modality. This is not about vanity, it is about **visibility**: truly seeing yourself, acknowledging your worth, and creating a new, embodied relationship with who you are. By returning to the mirror day after day, you are not only reprogramming your thoughts, you are **reclaiming your voice**, **rewriting your story**, and **rebuilding your identity** from the inside out.

### Mirror Work As A Daily Emotional Intelligence Ritual

Mirror work is more than just a moment in front of your reflection, it is a sacred ritual that invites you to reconnect with your inner self. When you look into your own eyes and speak words of affirmation or truth, you are choosing to see yourself with clarity, compassion, and courage. You give yourself permission to be fully seen, not just by the world, but by you. As a daily emotional intelligence ritual, mirror work helps you build **self-**

**awareness**. You begin to notice how you feel as you speak to yourself, how your body responds, and what thoughts arise. This awareness becomes a powerful guide, helping you better understand the emotional patterns that shape your life. You also develop **self-regulation**. As difficult emotions surface, like shame, fear, or self-doubt, you learn to sit with them, breathe through them, and respond with love instead of judgment. This daily practice teaches you how to pause, reflect, and choose kindness, even in moments of inner conflict. Your **motivation** is reignited. By affirming who you are and who you are becoming, you strengthen your commitment to live with purpose and integrity. You begin to show up for yourself in ways you once reserved only for others. **Self-compassion** deepens. Through consistent mirror work, you begin to soften toward yourself. You realise that the love, encouragement, and forgiveness you have offered others is something you deeply deserve too. You learn to be your own ally, and over time, your **emotional resilience** grows. You face yourself daily, with all your wounds and wisdom, and instead of turning away, you lean in. You find strength in your softness and courage in your honesty. When you practice mirror work regularly, you create space for healing, integration, and growth. You start each day by declaring: *I see you. I hear you. I am here for you,* and in doing so, you transform the mirror from a place of judgment into a sacred space of self-connection and heart-led transformation.

**The Three Phases Of Mirror Work**

***Awareness • Courage • Embodiment***

<u>1. Awareness - Meeting Yourself with Presence</u>

You begin by simply showing up. Standing in front of the mirror, you allow yourself to be seen, not just physically, but emotionally and energetically. You become aware of the stories you have been telling yourself, the critical thoughts that arise, the resistance in your body, and the way you have been avoiding your own gaze. This phase is about *honest observation.* You do not need to change anything, just notice. You are learning to witness yourself with curiosity rather than judgment.

<u>2. Courage - Leaning into Discomfort with Love</u>

It takes real bravery to stay. As you continue mirror work, emotions may surface, grief, anger, shame, or sadness. In this phase, you are called to *remain present* despite discomfort. You begin to say words that feel foreign, like "*I am enough*" or "*I am lovable,*" even if a part of you does not yet believe them. This is the work of the heart, stepping beyond old patterns and daring to believe in your own worth. Courage means trusting that you are safe to feel and safe to heal.

3. Embodiment - Living the Truth of Who You Are

Over time, what once felt difficult becomes natural. You begin to *live* your affirmations. You do not just say "*I am worthy*", you move through the world with that truth in your body. This is embodiment: when love, self-trust, and confidence move from thoughts into action. You find yourself making aligned choices, setting healthy boundaries, expressing your truth, and embracing your life with compassion and presence. You become a living mirror of the love you have discovered within.

**Why Facing Yourself Can Be So Confronting, And Liberating**

Facing yourself can feel like stepping into uncharted territory, because when you slow down and truly see yourself, without judgment or distraction, you come face-to-face with everything you have tried to suppress, avoid, or ignore. It can be deeply confronting because it invites you to witness not only your strengths and successes, but also your wounds, insecurities, regrets, and unmet needs. You might feel exposed, vulnerable, or even overwhelmed, because mirror work asks you to meet your inner world with honesty and compassion. You may hear the old narratives you have carried for years: *"I am not enough," "I am unlovable," "I failed."* These stories can be hard to confront, but when you do, you begin to reclaim your power. You learn that your worth is not defined by the past, by perfection, or by other people's opinions. You realise that your heart has always held the wisdom and strength to heal, and this is where the liberation begins. By facing yourself with presence and kindness, you open the door to deep emotional freedom. You stop running from who you are and start embracing every part of your being. In that reflection, you start to see not just flaws or pain, but your resilience, your capacity for love, and your divine potential. You give yourself permission to be human, to grow, to feel, to transform. This brave act of self-meeting does not just change how you see yourself. It changes how you live. It grounds you in authenticity, empowers your choices, and strengthens your relationships with others. The very mirror that once felt intimidating becomes a sacred space, a space where you come home to yourself, again and again.

**Mirror Exercise**

**Purpose:** To cultivate self-acceptance, dissolve limiting self-beliefs, and reconnect with your heart through the healing power of eye contact and affirmations.

**Step-by-Step Guide:**

1. **Find Your Mirror Space:** Choose a quiet, private space where you can stand or sit comfortably in front of a mirror. Make sure you will not be disturbed. Gently dim the lights if you wish to create a softer, heart-held atmosphere.
2. **Place Your Hand on Your Heart:** Take three slow, deep breaths. As you inhale, feel your chest rise. As you exhale, feel your body soften. Bring your awareness to your heart and place your hand over it.
3. **Look Into Your Eyes:** Gaze into your own eyes, not with judgment or critique, but with curiosity and tenderness. Allow yourself to simply *see* the person in the mirror.
4. **Speak the Following Affirmations Aloud (or Create Your Own):**
    1. *"I see you."*
    2. *"You are worthy of love."*
    3. *"I forgive you."*
    4. *"I am here for you."* **Repeat each one slowly. Pause between statements to breathe and feel.**
5. **Notice the Resistance or Emotion**

    Do not rush past discomfort. If tears come, let them flow. If resistance arises, acknowledge it gently: *"I see you, too."* You are meeting parts of yourself that have long been waiting to be held.
6. **Close with This Statement:**

    *"Every time I return to the mirror, I return to myself."*
7. **Journal Reflection (Optional):**

    Write about what you noticed, felt, resisted, or accepted during the practice.

This is not about perfection, it is about presence. Do this daily for one week and watch how your relationship with yourself transforms.

## Case Study Discussion: Michael's Journey

Michael was a larger-than-life character with an infectious personality. Michael was a self–made man in his mid-40s and anybody looking at Michael and his life would have been left with the impression that he was someone who was in a good place. However, this was not the case. Michael liked helping others, but his self–talk was brutal, and he did not love himself at all. I journeyed with Michael for quite a few months, and we did some deep healing. One of the things I requested of Michael was to feel into his heart and make a list of all the things he truly loved about himself. Over time this list grew, and I asked Michael to read his list out loud to himself in front of a mirror. I still recall the conversation I had with Michael after I asked him to read his list to himself in front of the mirror. His response, '*there is no f…n way I am reading anything out to myself in front of the mirror.*' The mere thought of this terrified him. Michael had conditioned himself over decades to believe that he was wholly unworthy, an imposter. I then asked Michael to read his list to me over our Zoom call and he did. I then asked him to just stand in front of his mirror for 60 seconds every day for a week and say nothing. Michael agreed, and over the next 6 months Michael found the courage to take small steps, to heal, learn and grow. He got to a point where he could face himself in the mirror, speak out loud and truly believe the words he was saying.

*(Authors note: Please note that every person is different, and every person has different hurts, pains, woundings and traumas. The point I would like you take from Michael's story is to never give up on yourself. You are a precious gift, and your life is to be lived and not merely survived. Living an authentic life off integrity is more than just existing!)*

**Reflective Exercise: Michael's Journey**

Here are four profound and reflective questions to help you deeply engage with Michael's story and the power of mirror work:

1. **When you look into the mirror, what is the first thought or feeling that arises, and is it truly yours, or a reflection of someone else's voice from your past?** *This question invites you to notice old programming and become aware of whose expectations or judgments you have internalised.*
2. **What part of yourself have you struggled to face, and what might happen if you chose to meet that part with compassion instead**

**of criticism?** *This encourages emotional courage and opens the door to deep self-acceptance and healing.*

3. **How has avoiding your own gaze affected your relationship with yourself and others?** *This helps you explore the link between self-awareness and how authentically you connect with the world around you.*
4. **If you could speak one truth into the mirror that your younger self longed to hear, what would it be, and how would it change the way you live today?** *This helps you engage in self-reparenting and step into a more empowered, heart-led identity.*

### Affirmations For Integration (Heart Whispers)

Affirmations have the power to quiet the noise of doubt, open the doorway to self-trust, and draw you back into the wisdom of your heart. When practised daily, they nurture an inner dialogue based in love and truth, helping you live each day more aligned with who you truly are. I invite you to repeat silently or write:

- *I use the mirror to practice positive self–talk.*
- *I avoid judging myself when I look in the mirror.*
- *I find peace when I meditate in front of a mirror.*
- *I see my progress in my reflection during workouts.*
- *I remind myself of my worthiness when looking in the mirror.*
- *I honour the person I see in the mirror as a work in progress and a work of art.*
- *I embrace my reflection as a true expression of my authentic self.*
- *I look into the mirror and recognise the strength within me.*
- *I celebrate the unique beauty that is mine alone.*
- *I use my reflection as a reminder of how far I have come.*

**Mirror Exercise – Meeting Yourself with Love**

1. **Find Your Mirror:** Stand or sit comfortably in front of a mirror. Look directly into your own eyes.
2. **Breathe and Soften:** Take three slow, deep breaths. With each exhale, release any tension in your shoulders, jaw, or chest.

3. **Speak Your Name:** Gently say your name out loud, as if greeting a dear friend.
4. **Affirm Your Worth:** Choose one phrase to repeat slowly three times, such as:
   - *I see you, and you are enough.*
   - *I love and accept you, exactly as you are.*
   - *You are worthy of kindness and joy.*
5. **Close with Gratitude:** Place your hand over your heart, smile softly, and thank yourself for showing up in this moment.

**Closing Reflection**

The mirror is not merely glass, it is a sacred space where your deepest truths await. Each time you meet your own eyes, you are offered an invitation: to see beyond the surface and witness the essence of who you truly are. In this reflection, you face not only your image but the stories, wounds, and beliefs you have carried, some yours, some not. It takes courage to look and even more to stay, but as you soften your gaze and open your heart, what once felt confronting becomes liberating. You begin to see not what is wrong with you, but what has always been right, your resilience, your beauty, your worth. Through mirror work, you reclaim the power to rewrite your inner narrative.

- *You unlearn shame.*
- *You meet your pain with tenderness.*
- *You awaken self-compassion, and gradually, you return home to yourself.*

May your mirror become a place of presence, healing, and truth, and may you always remember: the reflection you see is not just who you are, it is who you are becoming.

**Keep Walking the Unbound Way**

You are not meant to do this work alone. There are more practices, more modules, more companions, and more guidance waiting across the Unbound Series and its programs. When you are ready, take the next stride – www.timetotransform.world

# MODULE 4 – GROUNDING

**Your Opening Reflection**

**Invitation to Grounding** - As you step into this module, I invite you to let the earth beneath you hold your weight, steady and sure. Imagine roots extending from your body into the ground, reminding you that you are supported, anchored, and safe. This is your moment to return to yourself, to release the rush, to soften the tension, and to remember that you are never separate from the strength and stability of the earth. Breathe deeply, feel your presence, and allow yourself to come home to your grounding.

- "When was the last time you felt fully anchored, steady, and safe in yourself?"
- "What practices, people, or places help you return to a sense of grounded calm when life feels overwhelming?"
- "In what areas of your life do you feel scattered or unsteady, and what might help you ground more deeply there?"
- "How does your body tell you when you are grounded, what sensations, rhythms, or signals arise?"
- "What does it mean to you to stand firmly in your truth, no matter what storms arise around you?"

Let these questions open the doorway into presence. Every answer you give, whether in words, sensations, or silence, is a bridge between where you are and where you are going.

**Learning Objectives**

The learning objectives are included here to give you a clear focus for this module, ensuring that each practice you explore moves you closer to mastering the skills, insights, and heart-led awareness that will enrich your life well beyond the program. By the end of this module, you will:

- Understand the emotional and physiological benefits of grounding.
- Learn and experience grounding techniques to reduce anxiety and stress.
- Deepen self-awareness by reconnecting with the physical body and present moment.
- Recognise grounding as a tool for emotional regulation and decision-making.
- Integrate grounding practices into daily life for ongoing balance and heart connection.

**Core Emotional Domains**

The core emotional intelligence domains covered here are essential because they form the foundation for lasting heart connection, guiding you to deepen self-awareness, regulate emotions, build resilience, and strengthen the mind-body bond throughout your *Unbound* journey.

- **Self-Awareness:** Grounding anchors you in the present moment, helping you notice your thoughts, sensations, and emotions as they arise.
- **Self-Regulation:** By connecting with your body and breath, you calm your nervous system and create space to respond rather than react.
- **Emotional Resilience:** Grounding builds inner stability, allowing you to navigate stress and uncertainty with greater clarity and strength.
- **Empathy:** When you are grounded, you are more attuned to others, your presence becomes deeper, and compassion flows with ease and authenticity *"Forgiveness - Releasing The Past"*

**"Grounding – Finding Safety in the Present"**

<u>Grounding: Coming Home to the Body, the Moment, and Yourself</u>

Grounding is both a **physical** and **emotional** process, a returning to what is real, stable, and present. In a world that often pulls you into the past with regret or into the future with anxiety, grounding gently invites you back into the *now*. It reminds you that safety, clarity, and calm are found not in racing thoughts, but in the stillness beneath them. When you ground yourself, you **anchor into your body**, your breath, your senses. You notice the earth beneath your feet, the rise and fall of your chest, the sounds and textures around you. This simple act of presence creates an immediate shift: your mind begins to settle, your nervous system calms, and the storm of emotion begins to soften. Emotionally, grounding is a tool for **self-regulation**. It helps you find your centre when you feel overwhelmed, disconnected, or scattered. It allows you to respond with intention rather than react from fear or fatigue. In this grounded state, you are more resilient, more clear, and more compassionate, with yourself and with others. Grounding is not about escaping your experience, it is about **embodying it fully**, without judgment. It teaches you that peace is not the absence of challenge, but the presence of groundedness. In grounding, you come back to yourself.

- To breath.
- To presence.
- To the steady truth that **this moment is enough,** and so are you.

**What Is Grounding?**

Across time and tradition, grounding has been more than a calming technique, it has been a sacred relationship between your human spirit and the living Earth. Long before science named the nervous system or psychology defined trauma, cultures around the world understood that healing begins by returning to the ground beneath you.

<u>Indigenous Traditions: Grounding as Relationship and Reverence</u>

In many Indigenous cultures, grounding is a deeply spiritual act, one of **connection, reciprocity, and respect** for the Earth as a living, breathing being. The land is not a resource to be used, but a relative to be honoured. Through practices such as walking barefoot, smudging, drumming, or placing hands on trees, grounding becomes a way of **coming back to wholeness,** not just as individuals, but as part of a greater web of life. The Earth is seen as a **source of wisdom and nourishment**, holding memory, energy, and guidance. When you feel overwhelmed, lost, or fragmented, you are often invited to "*go back to the land*", to sit in silence, feel the soil, listen to the wind, or immerse yourself in ceremony. These are not passive acts of escape, but intentional pathways to **embodied remembrance**. Grounding in this context is about restoring **right relationship,** with the self, with community, and with the more-than-human world. It is about listening with your feet, breathing with the trees, and remembering that **you belong**.

Ayurveda and Traditional Chinese Medicine: Grounding as Energetic Balance

In **Ayurveda**, grounding is associated with the **root chakra** (*Muladhara*), the energetic centre located at the base of your spine, which governs your sense of safety, stability, and survival. When this chakra is balanced, you feel **secure, present, and anchored**. When imbalanced, you may feel anxious, scattered, or disconnected. Practices like **prāṇāyāma** (breath control), restorative yoga, warm foods, daily rituals, and time in nature are used to stabilise and nourish your root chakra, reconnecting you with your body and the rhythms of the Earth. In **Traditional Chinese Medicine**, grounding is tied to the **Earth element**, which governs digestion, nourishment, and emotional equilibrium. When the Earth element is strong, it offers inner centredness and clarity. Grounding practices in this tradition often include **qigong**, **earthing exercises**, **tai chi**, and mindful eating, methods that restore **harmony between body, emotion, and environment**.

Monastic and Contemplative Traditions: Grounding as Inner Stillness

In Christian, Buddhist, and other monastic traditions, grounding was cultivated through **structured ritual and silent practice**. Walking meditations in cloisters, the rhythm of chanting, breath-focused prayers like the *Jesus Prayer*, and time in nature were all ways of **stilling the mind and rooting the soul**. These practices were not escapes from the world, but portals into the **inner sanctuary of presence**. Grounding in this context became a **spiritual discipline,** a path to humility, surrender, and alignment with the divine.

A Shared Wisdom

Across all these traditions, grounding was never just a practice. It was a **return,** to the Earth, to the self, to the sacred. It reminds you that healing is not about striving upward, but about **deepening downward.**

- That clarity is not always in thinking more, but in **feeling more**.
- That strength is found not in resistance, but in **groundedness**.

Grounding invites you to come back to what has always held you: ***The Earth. Your breath. The moment. Your body. Your truth.***

Modern Psychological and Somatic Approaches to Grounding

*Healing the Mind by Reconnecting to the Body*

In modern psychology, particularly in trauma-informed, somatic, and mindfulness-based practices, **grounding is now understood as a vital and evidence-based strategy** for emotional regulation, safety, and mental clarity. It has become a cornerstone of therapeutic interventions for anxiety, trauma, dissociation, and chronic stress, not just as a coping mechanism, but as a pathway to long-term healing.

What Is Grounding in Psychological Terms?

Grounding refers to any technique that brings your awareness back into the *present moment* by reconnecting you with your body, breath, senses, and surroundings. When a person is emotionally overwhelmed, by stress, anxiety, trauma triggers, or intrusive thoughts, the brain can easily slip into **fight, flight, freeze, or fawn** responses. Grounding interrupts this physiological cascade by helping you regulate your nervous system and re-engage with safety. Common techniques include:

- **Breathwork** (e.g., extended exhale, box breathing)
- **Sensory orientation** (e.g., the 5-4-3-2-1 method)
- **Movement** (e.g., walking, stretching, shaking out tension)
- **Touch-based techniques** (e.g., holding a warm mug, pressing your feet into the floor)
- **Visualisation** (e.g., imagining roots growing from your feet into the earth)

These practices help shift attention **from spiraling thoughts into embodied awareness**, creating an internal pause, just long enough to access clarity, resilience, and self-agency.

The Neuroscience Behind Grounding

From a neurological perspective, grounding activates your **parasympathetic nervous system**, also known as the *"rest-and-digest"* system. This calms the stress response (regulated by your sympathetic nervous system), lowering cortisol and adrenaline levels, slowing the heart rate, and stabilising blood pressure. By drawing awareness back to the present moment, grounding can interrupt your neural pathways associated with trauma flashbacks or rumination. It also engages your **prefrontal cortex**, your brain's centre for reasoning, planning, and self-regulation, restoring executive function after emotional flooding. In short, grounding supports **neuroplasticity,** your brain's ability to rewire and recover from dysregulation, by building new, safer associations with embodiment and presence.

The Somatic Approach: Reclaiming the Wisdom of the Body

Somatic therapists recognise that trauma is not only a psychological wound, it is stored in your **nervous system and the body**. Grounding becomes a way for you to **return safely to your body**, especially if you have dissociated from it due to past pain or overwhelm. Rather than analysing thoughts or reliving traumatic memories, somatic grounding gently guides you to feel your feet on the floor, your breath in your chest, or your spine rising with strength. These micro-moments of safety begin to re-establish trust in your body's ability to hold experience without collapsing under it. This work is especially powerful in helping you move from **numbness to aliveness**, from **hyperarousal to regulation**, and from **survival to embodiment**.

From Coping Skill to Healing Practice

While grounding is often introduced as a short-term coping technique, its **long-term practice opens a doorway to deeper healing**. As you develop a daily grounding rhythm, whether through meditation, nature walks, sensory awareness, or movement, you begin to feel more grounded, more spacious, and more connected. This shift allows emotional experiences to **flow rather than flood**, making space for self-compassion, insight, and transformation. In a world that can often feel chaotic, fast-paced, and overstimulating, grounding becomes more than a practice, it becomes a way of being. *A quiet return to presence. A place of inner safety. A daily commitment to coming home to yourself.*

### Benefits of Grounding: Physical Health, and Emotional Clarity

Grounding is more than a calming technique, it is a **holistic practice** that supports your wellbeing on multiple levels. When you ground yourself, you return to your natural state of presence: a place where your body feels safe, your emotions are balanced, and your spirit is attuned to its deeper wisdom. Let us explore how grounding nurtures **your whole self**:

Physical Health: Regulating the Nervous System and Energising the Body

At its core, grounding supports **physiological equilibrium,** helping your body return to a natural state of balance after the wear and tear of chronic stress, overstimulation, or emotional overload. In today's fast-paced world, many people live in a prolonged state of **sympathetic nervous system dominance**, also known as the **fight, flight, or freeze** response. This can lead to fatigue, insomnia, digestive issues, inflammation, and suppressed immune function. Grounding counteracts this by **activating the parasympathetic nervous system,** your body's built-in *rest, digest, and restore* mode. This shift results in a cascade of positive physiological effects:

1. **Lowered Heart Rate and Blood Pressure**: As your body begins to feel safe and supported, your cardiovascular system relaxes. Grounding helps reduce the physical markers of stress, allowing your heart to beat more steadily and efficiently.
2. **Improved Sleep and Circadian Rhythm**: Grounding practices, especially those performed in nature or with intentional breath, help regulate melatonin production and rebalance disrupted sleep cycles. When you are grounded, your body re-attunes to its natural rhythms, making rest deeper and more restorative.
3. **Reduced Cortisol Levels**: Chronic stress elevates cortisol, which over time can contribute to weight gain, mood swings, inflammation, and immune suppression. Grounding has been shown to reduce cortisol production, allowing the body to repair and regenerate more effectively.
4. **Enhanced Energy and Vitality**: When your nervous system is calm and balanced, more energy is available for life. Grounding clears internal tension, improves oxygenation, and restores clarity, leading to increased stamina and a greater sense of aliveness throughout the day.

<u>Earthing: Grounding with the Earth Itself</u>

In recent years, scientific studies on ***"earthing"*****,** the direct physical connection with the Earth's surface, have brought new insight into ancient practices. Research indicates that **barefoot contact with soil, sand, grass, or natural stone** allows the body to absorb negatively charged electrons from the Earth, which may help:

- Reduce systemic **inflammation**
- Improve **immune function**
- Normalise **blood viscosity**
- Support **electromagnetic balance** in the body

While more research is emerging, many report subjective benefits such as quicker recovery from fatigue, improved mood, and reduced physical pain after regular time spent connecting physically with the Earth. Even a few minutes a day, **feet in the grass, hands on a tree, or sitting quietly outdoors,** can have cumulative and profound health effects.

## Grounding And Emotional Intelligence: Enhancing Presence And Choice

When you ground yourself, you give your emotional intelligence the space it needs to grow. Grounding is not just about calming down, it is about **coming back to yourself** so you can respond to life with clarity rather than react from stress or fear. In moments of overwhelm, your nervous system can hijack your thoughts and actions. You might feel scattered, reactive, or disconnected, but when you pause, take a breath, feel your feet on the floor, and **anchor into your body**, you interrupt that automatic pattern. You return to the present moment, and with that presence comes **the power to choose** how you show up. Grounding deepens your **self-awareness** by helping you notice what you are actually feeling, not just what you are thinking. It supports **self-regulation**, allowing you to move from reaction to reflection. When you are grounded, you are more likely to pause before speaking, to listen deeply, and to respond with compassion, toward yourself and others. This grounded awareness enhances **empathy**, **resilience**, and **relational intelligence**. You are no longer swept away by the noise around you; you stand in the calm centre of your own truth. From that place, you can lead, connect, and live with integrity and emotional clarity. Every time you ground yourself, you reclaim choice, and with choice comes freedom, power, and presence.

## The Neuroscience Of Stress And How Grounding Activates The Parasympathetic Nervous System

When you are under stress, whether from a deadline, an emotional trigger, a conflict, or even an old memory, your body responds instantly. Without you needing to think about it, your brain signals your nervous system to protect you. You may feel your heart race, your breath quicken, your muscles tighten, or your thoughts spiral. This is your **sympathetic nervous system** kicking in: the part of your body designed to keep you alive through the **fight, flight, or freeze response**. This response is meant for short bursts of danger, but in your modern world, threats are not always physical. They are emotional, relational, digital, or imagined, and they can last all day. If you do not reset, your nervous system can stay stuck in overdrive. This is when you feel burned out, anxious, overwhelmed, disconnected, or numb. Here is the good news:

**your body also has a built-in healing mechanism,** your **parasympathetic nervous system**. This is your **rest, digest, and restore** mode. It slows your heart rate, deepens your breath, supports digestion, improves immune function, and calms your brain. When you ground yourself, you send a new signal to your brain: *"It is okay. I am safe now."* You do this by bringing your awareness back into your body:

- You feel your feet on the floor.
- You take a slow, intentional breath.
- You notice the sensation of your hand on your chest or belly.
- You orient your senses. What can you see, hear, feel?

These small acts may seem simple, but they **rewire your brain**. They activate your **prefrontal cortex,** the part of your mind responsible for awareness, compassion, decision-making, and self-regulation. When you ground yourself, you do not bypass stress, you **transform your relationship to it**. You become the calm in the storm. You reconnect with your body as a safe place, not just a container for tension, and from that calm space, you can think more clearly, feel more honestly, and choose how to move forward, on your terms. So the next time life feels too much, pause:

1. Ground yourself.
2. Feel your breath.
3. Feel the Earth beneath you.

Remember, you are not stuck in stress. You have the power to return to safety, clarity, and strength. This is the neuroscience of self-empowerment. This is the wisdom of grounding in action.

### Integrating Grounding Into High-Performance Environments And Daily Rituals

Grounding is not just something you turn to in a crisis, it is a practice you can weave into the rhythm of your day, especially in **high-performance environments** where focus, clarity, and emotional balance are essential. Whether you are leading a team, presenting to stakeholders, managing clients, or studying under pressure, you are constantly being asked to perform, decide, and respond, and while your mind may be sharp, your **nervous system needs stability** to sustain excellence without burnout. That is where grounding becomes your secret edge. When you integrate grounding into your daily rituals, you begin to **regulate your energy, sharpen your attention, and increase your emotional intelligence,** even in demanding situations.

Start with Small Anchors Throughout the Day

You do not need hours of meditation or a quiet retreat to ground yourself. You can build **micro-moments of reconnection** into your day:

- **Before a meeting** – Take 3 slow breaths. Feel your feet on the floor. Say quietly, *"I am present."*
- **When giving feedback** – Place one hand over your chest or stomach. Speak from grounded clarity, not reactivity.
- **After back-to-back calls or emails** – Stand, stretch, and breathe. Let the tension leave your shoulders and jaw.
- **At the start of your day** – Write a short intention like: *"I choose calm under pressure."*

These rituals do not interrupt performance, they **sustain it**. When you are grounded, you do not rush decisions. You do not get easily hijacked by stress. You speak with authority **without losing empathy**.

Why It Works in High-Performance Settings

Grounding activates your **prefrontal cortex**, allowing you to make smarter, more emotionally balanced decisions under pressure. It also quiets the noise of fear, perfectionism, and urgency, so you can lead, communicate, and execute with clarity. The more you practice, the more you train your nervous system to come back to balance quickly. Over time, you become the kind of person who can stay **calm in the storm**, adapt with grace, and lead others by your presence, not just your position.

Grounding as a Leadership and Lifestyle Practice

When you integrate grounding into your lifestyle, it is no longer just a tool, it becomes a way of being. You begin to show up **more present in your relationships, more attentive with your teams**, and **more connected to your own needs**. Grounding becomes the space between stimulus and response. It becomes your reset button, your pause, your return, and in high-performance environments, that makes all the difference. So whether you are navigating deadlines, studying under pressure, leading meetings, or managing emotional complexity, come back to your breath. Come back to your body.

**Come back to the ground beneath you.**

**Sensory Awareness Walk (Outdoor or Simulated)**

I invite you to:

1. Walk slowly, paying close attention to the sensations in your feet, the pressure, texture, and rhythm of each step.
2. Tune into the sounds, smells, and textures around you, allowing each sense to awaken fully.
3. At intervals, pause, close your eyes if comfortable, and take three deep grounding breaths, feeling your body anchored in the present moment.

**Debrief:** After your walk, take a few minutes to reflect: *What emotions or insights emerged during your walk? How did your body feel? What changed in your mind or heart?*

**Case Study Discussion: Lucas's Journey**

After a lifetime of working long hours as a long–haul truck driver, and always being on the go, Lucas found himself in a state of constant stress and anxiety. He had tried everything from medication to therapy, but nothing seemed to work. One day, Lucaș contacted me and after 3–4 weeks I chatted with him about trying grounding. I asked Lucas to connect with the earth's natural energy by walking barefoot or lying on the ground. At first, Lucas was highly skeptical, but he decided to give it a try. Lucas took off his shoes and walked on the grass in his backyard, feeling the cool blades between his toes. As he walked, he focused on his breath and let his mind clear. He felt a sense of calm and peace within him that he had not experienced in years. From that day forward, Lucas made grounding a daily practice. He spent time in nature, whether it was walking barefoot on the beach or lying in a park. Lucas found that his stress and anxiety levels decreased significantly, and he felt more balanced and centred in his life. He also discovered that grounding had other benefits. He felt more connected to the world around him and more in tune with his own emotions (this was massive for Lucas). Lucas began to appreciate the small moments of beauty and joy that he had previously overlooked. He felt more present in the moment and was able to connect with others on a deeper level. He also found that he had more energy and focus for the things that truly mattered to him. Lucas realised that grounding was not a cure–all, but it was an important tool in his toolbox for managing stress and anxiety. It was something that he could always turn to when he needed to find balance in his life.

**Reflective Exercise: Lucas's Journey**

Here are four profound and reflective questions inspired by Lucas's story to help you engage with your own grounding journey:

**1. When was the last time you allowed the earth to hold you, without rushing, fixing, or thinking?**

**Reflection:** Like Lucas, you may have spent much of your life in motion, driven by responsibility, pressure, or habit, but grounding reminds you that rest is not weakness; it is wisdom. When you let yourself slow down, even for a few moments, you invite in calm, clarity, and healing that your body has longed for.

**2. What would it feel like to reconnect with the ground beneath your feet, not just physically, but emotionally?**

**Reflection:** Your body knows how to return home to presence. Each breath, each barefoot step, each moment of stillness is a pathway back to your centre. When you take time to ground, you give your nervous system the safety it needs to regulate, and your heart the space it needs to soften.

**3. Where in your day do you most need a pause, a moment to breathe, feel, and return to yourself?**

**Reflection:** Lucas found that a few minutes barefoot in the grass changed everything. You do not need perfect conditions, just a willingness to pause. These micro-moments of grounding can become sacred rituals that restore your energy, reduce anxiety, and remind you that you are not just surviving, you are allowed to feel alive.

**4. What might open up for you if you truly believed that you are supported, by the ground, by the moment, by life itself?**

**Reflection:** Grounding is not just a technique, it is a shift in trust. It is the quiet knowing that you do not have to carry everything alone. Just like Lucas, you can find stability not by gripping harder, but by surrendering to what's already holding you. The ground is always there. So is your breath. So are you.

**Affirmations For Integration: (Heart Whispers)**

Affirmations have the power to quiet the noise of doubt, open the doorway to self-trust, and draw you back into the wisdom of your heart. When practised daily, they nurture an inner dialogue based in love and truth, helping you live each day more aligned with who you truly are. I invite you to repeat silently or write:

- *I feel more centred and calmer after grounding exercises.*
- *I notice a decrease in anxiety when I practice grounding.*
- *I am more in tune with my body when I ground myself.*
- *I find it easier to focus on the present moment with grounding.*
- *I feel more connected to the earth when I practice grounding.*
- *I release tension more easily when I practice grounding.*
- *Grounding helps me respond to challenges with greater clarity and patience.*
- *My thoughts feel more organised and steady after grounding.*
- *Grounding reconnects me to my inner strength and stability.*

**Optional Extension Activity**

Here are **3 original grounding exercises**. Each exercise includes **three parts,** a physical action, a mindful practice, and a heart-centred integration:

**Exercise 1: Tree Lean + Grounding Intention + Heart Touch**

**1. Tree Lean:** Stand or sit with your back gently resting against a tree or solid wall. Feel the support behind you and allow your body to relax into it. Let the earth carry your weight.

**2. Grounding Intention:** Silently repeat an intention such as: *"I am safe. I am supported. I am here."* Let this intention settle into your body like roots beneath the surface.

**3. Heart Touch:** Place one hand on your heart and the other on your belly. Breathe slowly. With each breath, invite yourself to feel grounded, present, and connected to the now.

**Exercise 2: Stone Hold + Stillness Scan + Anchoring Phrase**

**1. Stone Hold:** Find a small stone or natural object. Hold it in your palm and observe its weight, texture, and temperature. Let it represent steadiness in your life.

**2. Stillness Scan:** Close your eyes and scan your body slowly from head to toe. Notice where tension lives and where ease flows. Stay curious, not critical.

**3. Anchoring Phrase:** Repeat quietly: *"In this moment, I return to myself."* Feel the energy of the stone and your breath grounding you into your inner calm.

**Exercise 3: Spiral Walk + Sensory Awareness + Grounded Statement**

**1. Spiral Walk:** Mark a small spiral pattern in the sand, grass, or with objects. Slowly walk the spiral path inward. With each step, let go of distraction or stress.

**2. Sensory Awareness:** Pause in the centre. Tune into 3 things you can feel, 3 sounds you can hear, and 3 natural elements around you. Let your senses awaken presence.

**3. Grounded Statement:** Say softly to yourself: *"I am grounded. I belong to this earth. I am at peace."* Then walk the spiral path back out with renewed focus.

**Closing Reflection**

As you come to the end of this part of your journey, remember: grounding is not something outside of you, it is within you, always. When life feels too fast, too loud, or too much, you can pause. You can feel your breath. You can feel the ground beneath your feet. You are **not** lost. You are not disconnected. You are simply being called back to the place you never truly left, **your body, your breath, your being**. Grounding is a quiet act of power. It brings you back into the present, where peace begins, where clarity returns, where your heart can speak again. No matter what is happening around you, you now have a way to return home to yourself. So take this with you:

- You are safe to pause.
- You are safe to feel.
- You are safe to come back to now.

Let every step forward be grounded in presence. Let every breath remind you, you are here, and that is enough.

**The Path Opens Further**

You have taken a step. The next step is waiting. Every book in the Unbound Series widens the path, deeper into your story, sharper into your strengths, and closer to the life you were meant to live.When you are ready, turn the page into the next Unbound journey – www.timetotransform.world

Time To Transform

EMPOWERING LIVES

Excellence in Practice

Part 2

# PART 2 – MOVE INTO EXCELLENCE IN PRACTICE

## (Time to Transform: Living Unbound - Chapters 14 Neurolinguistics • 15 Compassion • 25 Listening • 26 Focus)

Legal excellence is not produced by intelligence alone. It is produced by *how* intelligence is applied under pressure, in language chosen, attention held, power exercised, and judgment expressed. This section is concerned with that application. It is where the inner steadiness developed in Section One is translated into professional conduct. The four moduless in this section, **Neurolinguistics, Compassion, Listening, and Focus**, were selected because they shape the *quality of practice itself.* They govern how lawyers influence, persuade, negotiate, advise, and lead in environments where stakes are high and emotions are often unspoken but decisive. This is where craft becomes conscious.

### Why These Modules Matter in Legal Practice

**Neurolinguistics** addresses the fact that law is fundamentally a language-based profession. Lawyers influence outcomes not only through argument, but through framing, tone, sequencing, and word choice. Under stress, language often becomes sharper, narrower, or more adversarial than intended. This module develops awareness of how language shapes perception, in clients, courts, colleagues, and opponents, and how deliberate communication can de-escalate conflict, build trust, and increase persuasive power without aggression. For lawyers, this is not about manipulation. It is about responsibility in the use of language.

**Compassion** is included because legal work is saturated with human consequence. Clients rarely arrive at lawyers in neutral emotional states. They arrive in crisis, conflict, fear, or grief. Without compassion, lawyers risk becoming either detached technicians or emotionally over-invested advocates. This module clarifies compassion as a professional capacity, the ability to remain humane without losing boundaries, and to acknowledge impact without absorbing it. In practice, compassion improves judgment, strengthens client relationships, and reduces burnout. Compassion here is not sentiment. It is discernment applied to people.

**Listening** is one of the most underestimated legal skills. Lawyers are trained to speak persuasively. They are less often trained to listen with depth. Yet effective listening reveals what is not yet articulated, the interests beneath positions, the fears beneath demands, the risks beneath silence. This module refines listening as a deliberate practice that improves negotiation, advocacy, leadership, and conflict resolution. In law, what is unheard often matters as much as what is said.

**Focus** addresses the cognitive reality of modern legal work. Fragmentation, constant interruption, and digital overload erode the quality of thinking required for complex legal tasks. Focus is not merely productivity; it is the protection of professional judgment. This module restores disciplined attention, enabling lawyers to think deeply, decide carefully, and act deliberately, even in environments designed to fracture concentration. Together, these four modules create a professional posture that is **precise, humane, and effective**.

**When to Work With This Section**

This section is particularly relevant when you need to:

- negotiate, mediate, influence, or persuade without force
- handle difficult clients, opposing counsel, or internal tension
- communicate clearly when pressure is high and time is limited
- maintain concentration and performance in complex or fragmented environments
- lead teams, matters, or conversations that require both authority and restraint

These are not exceptional moments in legal life. They are routine, and they are decisive.

## The Deeper Purpose of Section Two

In legal practice, power is unavoidable. Lawyers wield it through advice, advocacy, language, and decision-making. The question is not whether power is used, but *how*. Section Two exists to ensure that influence is exercised with awareness rather than habit, and authority with responsibility rather than reflex. It helps lawyers move from reactive practice, driven by urgency, emotion, or precedent alone, to intentional mastery grounded in presence, clarity, and ethical consideration. This is where the law is practised not only correctly, but well. Excellence here is not louder argument, sharper dominance, or greater control. It is precision with restraint, persuasion with integrity, and effectiveness without erosion of self or others.

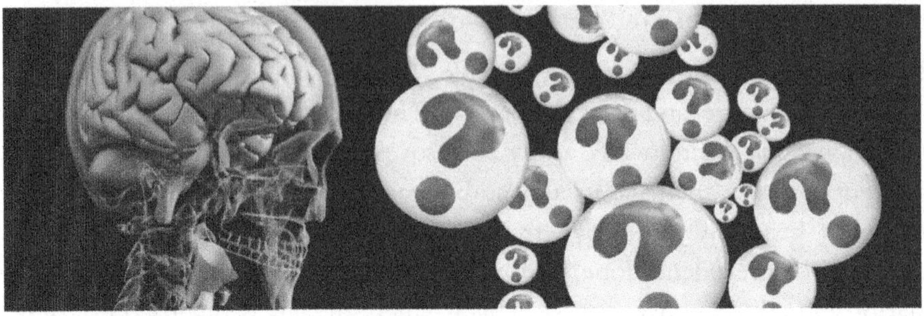

# MODULE 5 – NEUROLINGUISTICS

## Your Opening Reflection

**Invitation to Your Words** - As you begin this module, I invite you to listen closely to the language you carry within. Every word you speak, aloud or silently to yourself, is shaping your reality. This is your moment to pause and notice: are your words building you up or holding you back? Let this module be a gentle reminder that you have the power to rewrite your inner dialogue, to speak with kindness, and to call yourself into the fullness of who you truly are.

- "Are the words you use with yourself empowering you, or are they keeping you small?"
- "If your inner voice spoke to a friend, how would it sound, and would it be kind?"
- "What repeated phrases or stories shape the way you see yourself and the world?"
- "How might changing a single word you use with yourself shift your emotions, choices, or direction?"

Let these questions open the doorway into presence. Every answer you give, whether in words, sensations, or silence, is a bridge between where you are and where you are going.

## Learning Objectives

The learning objectives are included here to give you a clear focus for this module, ensuring that each practice you explore moves you closer to mastering the skills, insights, and heart-led awareness that will enrich your life well beyond the program. By the end of this module, you will:

- Understand the connection between language, thought, and emotion.
- Identify and challenge negative self-talk patterns.
- Apply neurolinguistic tools (like reframing, anchoring, and affirmations) to support emotional wellbeing.
- Cultivate heart-aligned communication within themselves and with others.

**Core Emotional Domains**

The core emotional intelligence domains covered here are essential because they form the foundation for lasting heart connection, guiding you to deepen self-awareness, regulate emotions, build resilience, and strengthen the mind-body bond throughout your *Unbound* journey.

- **Self-Awareness:** You begin to notice how your inner dialogue and spoken words shape your emotions, beliefs, and behaviours. Awareness of language becomes a mirror for your mind.
- **Self-Regulation:** By choosing more compassionate, empowering language, both internally and externally, you calm reactive patterns and open space for wiser responses.
- **Motivation:** Reframing your words fuels your inner drive. When your language aligns with your values and vision, motivation becomes heart-led and sustainable.
- **Empathy:** As you tune into the language of others with curiosity and presence, you hear more than just words, you feel intention, emotion, and unspoken needs.
- **Social Skills:** Conscious communication builds connection. With mindful language, you cultivate clarity, trust, and influence in your relationships, work, and leadership.

**"Neurolinguistics – Rewiring Your Thought Through Action"**

Neurolinguistics is a profound meeting point between language, neuroscience, and emotional intelligence. It reveals how the words you speak, especially the silent ones whispered in your own mind, shape the way your brain processes emotion, stores memory, and responds to the world around you. Every word you repeat, every label you attach to yourself, and every inner dialogue you rehearse either strengthens old emotional patterns or opens a doorway to new possibilities. When you begin to notice the language of your inner world, you unlock the power to rewire your emotional responses. A simple shift from *"I always fail"* to *"I am still learning"* is not just semantics, it is a neurological reset. That change in phrasing can ease your stress response, awaken curiosity, and open a pathway for growth. Words can constrict or expand, wound or heal, diminish or empower. They can trigger fear and shame, or they can ignite compassion, courage, and hope. By consciously choosing words that honor your heart's truth, words grounded in kindness, clarity, and self-belief, you begin reshaping not only your inner dialogue, but the lens through which you experience life. This is not about denying pain or pretending struggles do not exist. Rather, it is about reclaiming the power of interpretation, recognising that the language you choose creates the filter through which reality passes. Neurolinguistics is, at its essence, an invitation: to become the author of your story rather than a passive character in it. It asks you to align your mind with your heart, to speak to yourself with the same compassion you would offer someone you love. This intentional practice transforms not only how you engage with the world, but how you engage with yourself. When you change the words, you change the wiring. When you change the wiring, you change the story, and when you change the story, you change the life you live.

### A Brief History: Wernicke, Broca, Chomsky, And The Evolution Of Neurolinguistics

Neurolinguistics, as a field, sits at the fascinating crossroads of neuroscience, linguistics, psychology, and cognitive science. Its beginning can be traced back to the 19th century, when early pioneers began uncovering the relationship between the brain and language, an inquiry that would lay the foundation for understanding how words shape thought, emotion, and behavior.

**Paul Broca**, a French physician, was among the first to identify a specific region in the brain responsible for speech production. In the 1860s, he observed that patients with damage to the left frontal lobe, now known as *Broca's area,* struggled to speak fluently but could still comprehend language. His discovery established the revolutionary idea that different aspects of language are localised in specific brain regions.

Soon after, **Carl Wernicke**, a German neurologist, expanded on Broca's work. He discovered another key brain region, *Wernicke's area*, in the left temporal lobe, that is essential for understanding spoken language. Patients with damage here could speak in fluent but often nonsensical sentences, indicating a breakdown in comprehension. Together, Broca and Wernicke's findings laid the groundwork for the neurological study of language, giving rise to the concept of brain-based language networks.

In the 20th century, **Noam Chomsky** transformed the study of language with his theory of *universal grammar*. He proposed that the ability to acquire language is hardwired into the human brain, a biological capacity rather than just a learned behavior. While Chomsky focused more on theoretical linguistics than brain mechanisms, his work sparked new explorations into how language is structured and processed at the neurological level.

Modern neurolinguistics emerged as brain imaging technologies such as fMRI and EEG allowed researchers to observe the brain in action during language tasks. This has enabled deeper insights into how emotional language is encoded, how trauma and stress affect verbal processing, and how mindful language use can reshape neural patterns. Today, neurolinguistics not only explains how we speak and understand language, but also how language shapes emotion, identity, memory, and even our capacity for empathy and resilience. It underscores the profound truth that your words, both spoken and unspoken, are not merely tools of communication. They are reflections of your inner world and instruments for transforming it.

## How Language Creates Emotion: The Neuroscience Of Self-Talk

The language you use, especially your *self-talk*, does not just describe your reality; it **creates** it. Neuroscience now shows that your brain responds to internal language as if it were a lived experience. This means the words you silently repeat to yourself can directly influence your mood, shape your perception of self-worth, and even rewire your brain over time. When you engage in negative self-talk like "*I am a failure*" or "*I am not good enough*," your brain releases stress-related chemicals such as **cortisol** and **adrenaline**, activating the amygdala, your brain's fear centre. This can trigger a cascade of physiological responses: a racing heart, shallow breathing, and heightened anxiety. Over time, repeated negative language can carve deep neural grooves that reinforce low self-esteem, hopelessness, or shame. In contrast, compassionate and affirming self-talk like "*I am learning*," "*I am doing my best*," or "*I am enough*" activates the **prefrontal cortex,** the part of your brain responsible for conscious thought, emotional regulation, and long-term planning. It also stimulates the **release of oxytocin and serotonin**, neurochemicals associated with trust, well-being, and emotional resilience. Your brain does not distinguish much between language describing external reality and language directed inward. Telling yourself "*This is too hard*" sends the same stress signals as being under actual threat, but when you reframe with words like *"This is challenging, but I can grow through it,"* you engage more adaptive brain pathways, increasing your capacity to stay grounded, open, and motivated. In essence, your self-talk acts like a **neural script**, guiding your emotional responses, influencing decision-making, and shaping how you relate to yourself and others. The more conscious and kind your internal language becomes, the more emotionally intelligent and empowered your inner world grows. You have the power to change your brain, and your life, by changing your words.

## The Role Of Subconscious Programming In Emotional Patterns

The role of **subconscious programming** in emotional patterns is both profound and largely invisible, yet it influences nearly every aspect of your daily life. From the way you respond to conflict, to how you process love, failure, or success, your subconscious mind is constantly shaping your emotional experience through deeply embedded scripts and beliefs. Most of your **emotional reactions are not consciously chosen**. They are programmed responses that have been conditioned over time, often from childhood experiences, cultural influences, and repeated patterns of thought or behaviour. These subconscious programs live beneath the surface of awareness, stored in the limbic brain and nervous system, and they **automatically activate** in response to triggers. For example, if you were repeatedly told as a child that expressing sadness was weak, you may now subconsciously suppress sadness as an adult, reacting with anger, avoidance, or numbness instead. This is not a moral failing; it is a survival adaptation encoded into your subconscious for protection. Your subconscious mind operates like a **powerful emotional operating system**, running 95% of your daily thoughts, feelings, and behaviours. It governs how safe you feel in the world, how worthy you believe you are of love or success, and how you emotionally regulate in times of stress. The good news is that **subconscious programming is not fixed, it can be rewritten.** With intentional practices such as mindfulness, breathwork, neurolinguistic reprogramming, affirmations, and therapeutic reflection, you can begin to gently interrupt limiting patterns and rewire the emotional responses that no longer serve you.

Every time you pause to question your internal dialogue, every time you choose a more loving word or a conscious breath, you are reprogramming your emotional patterning toward greater freedom, presence, and heart connection. By learning to **partner with your subconscious rather than be controlled by it**, you unlock the power to transform emotional habits into healing, resilience, and profound self-awareness.

## Introducing Heart-Aligned Reframing And Emotional Anchoring

Heart-aligned reframing and emotional anchoring are transformative tools that allow you to reshape your inner world through the conscious use of language, emotion, and intention. These practices combine the wisdom of neurolinguistics with emotional intelligence to help you create a more empowered, compassionate, and heart-centred internal dialogue.

### Heart-Aligned Reframing

Reframing is the practice of seeing a situation through a new lens, one that offers possibility, insight, and meaning rather than limitation or defeat. When this is done through the heart, it becomes *heart-aligned reframing,* a process not only of shifting thoughts, but of softening the emotional energy behind them. Instead of asking, *"Why is this happening to me?"* a heart-aligned reframe might be, *"What is this moment asking me to learn?"* Instead of *"I failed again,"* you shift to *"I am growing through this, and my worth is not defined by outcomes."* This kind of reframing integrates both emotional truth and deeper compassion. It does not bypass pain or challenge; it honors the heart's wisdom in how you respond. Over time, heart-aligned reframing strengthens your emotional regulation, increases self-awareness, and expands your ability to hold hope and clarity, even in difficulty.

### Emotional Anchoring

Emotional anchoring is the practice of associating a *positive emotional state* (like peace, confidence, or self-love) with a simple, repeatable trigger, such as a word, breath, gesture, or memory. Anchors help you *return* to the emotional states that serve you, especially when you are feeling overwhelmed, triggered, or disconnected. For example:

1. Gently placing your hand on your heart and saying the word *"safe"* while breathing slowly can become an anchor to calm.

2. Remembering a moment when you felt deeply loved and linking it to the phrase *"I am enough"* can reconnect you to worthiness during times of doubt.

Anchoring creates a bridge between your **conscious intention** and your **emotional reality**, allowing your nervous system to regulate and your heart to remain present.

Why This Matters

Together, heart-aligned reframing and emotional anchoring help you:

- Break free from automatic negative patterns.
- Build inner safety and emotional resilience.
- Speak to yourself with truth and tenderness.
- Create a consistent path back to your heart when life feels chaotic.

These tools are not about pretending everything is okay, they are about *remembering* that you have the power to shift your inner state, return to your values, and live each day more grounded in love, clarity, and emotional integrity. Every time you pause, reframe, and anchor in your heart, you, re not only healing old patterns, you are also creating new ones. Ones that honour your wholeness.

## The Inner Narrative: How Changing Your Words Changes Your World

The Inner Narrative: How Changing Your Words Changes Your World

Your inner narrative, the ongoing dialogue you have with yourself, shapes how you feel, what you believe, and ultimately, how you live. It is not just a stream of private thoughts. It is the architecture of your emotional world, the filter through which you interpret experiences, and the blueprint for your choices, your confidence, and your relationships. Words are not neutral. Neuroscience shows that the language you use activates neural pathways associated with emotions, memory, and physical responses. For example, when you silently repeat harsh, critical statements to yourself like *"I am a failure"* or *"I will never be good enough,"* your brain and body respond as though those statements are fact, triggering stress responses, emotional shutdown, or withdrawal, but when you begin to shift your inner language to something more heart-connected, such as *"I am learning"*, *"I am growing"*, or *"This moment is hard, but I am doing my best"*, you create new emotional outcomes: more calm, more hope, more resilience.

Changing your words does not mean denying pain or pretending to be positive all the time. It means choosing language that opens the door to compassion, curiosity, and courage, especially in the midst of struggle. For example:

- Instead of *"I have to get this perfect,"* try *"I am allowed to make progress, not perfection."*
- Instead of *"I am so stupid for doing that,"* try *"That was hard, and I will choose differently next time."*
- Instead of *"No one cares,"* try *"I can reach out, I am not alone."*

These simple shifts create powerful emotional results.

- They guide your nervous system back to safety.
- They expand your tolerance for discomfort.
- They help you rewire old beliefs that may have been basecd in fear, shame, or survival.

Most importantly, they return you to your heart, and when your inner narrative becomes a place of support rather than self-sabotage, you begin to live with greater intention and emotional clarity. You make choices from wholeness, not wounding. You begin to create a world, not just outside of you, but within you, that reflects your truth, your worth, and your deep capacity for transformation. **Your words create your world. Speak to yourself the way you would to someone you love. Your heart is listening.**

**Neurolinguistic Heart Practice Toolkit Exercise**

This week, I invite you to choose **2 out of 5 neurolinguistic practices** to try. These simple but powerful tools help you reshape the language of your mind and heart, shifting patterns of thought and emotion into new possibilities for growth and healing.

**Reframing a Current Stressor**

- Choose a challenge you are facing right now. Write down how you usually describe or think about it.

- Then, create **three alternative interpretations** that bring light, learning, or opportunity into the situation.
- Example: Instead of "*This is too hard,*" reframe as "*This is teaching me resilience,*" or "*I am growing stronger through this.*"
- Notice how your body and emotions shift when you choose a new frame.

**Daily Affirmation Practice**

- Begin each day with a sentence of truth and encouragement that speaks to your heart.
- Examples: *"I am worthy of love and peace,"* or *"I grow stronger every time I choose kindness."*
- Say your affirmation out loud, write it in your journal, or place it somewhere visible.
- Over time, these affirmations begin to overwrite limiting self-talk.

**Anchoring a Positive State**

- Choose a physical gesture (e.g., tapping your heart, pressing your palms together, or holding your hand to your chest).
- Each time you feel gratitude, joy, or calm, pair the feeling with your chosen gesture.
- This builds a neurological *"anchor,"* so that over time, simply using the gesture can help you return to that positive state, even in moments of stress.

**Mirror Work – Speaking Compassion**

- Each day, stand in front of a mirror and speak a kind and compassionate truth to yourself.
- Examples: *"I am doing my best, and that is enough,"* or *"I forgive myself and choose to move forward with love."*
- At first, this may feel uncomfortable, but with repetition, it becomes a profound tool for rewiring self-image and self-talk.

**Visualisation – The Empowered Self**

- Take three minutes each morning to close your eyes and imagine yourself as the emotionally empowered version of you.
- See yourself calm, confident, and aligned with your heart. Notice how you walk, speak, and respond to life.

Let this image guide you throughout the day, reminding you that you are capable of stepping into this reality now.

**Case Study Discussion: Ingrid's Journey**

Ingrid was a vibrant and curious 68–year–old woman who had always been a seeker of knowledge and personal growth. She had a big, beautiful heart which she shared with others, but she generally kept people at arm's length, and we spent a lot of time focusing on her view of Self. Ingrid knew that the way she talked to herself, her 'self–talk', had a profound impact on her emotions and overall well–being. It was not compassionate, kind or nurturing, although she wanted it to be. It was for others but not for herself. Ingrid embarked on a journey of self–discovery and self–transformation. She really immersed herself in books, completed all my hearting exercises I set her and completed my heart of Life Series of programs. Through her exploration, Ingrid learned that her self–talk was often negative and self–critical. She discovered that these patterns of thought were based in past experiences and conditioning. Empowered with her newfound awareness, Ingrid began to challenge and reframe her self–talk. Whenever self–doubt or self–criticism arose, Ingrid consciously shifted her inner dialogue. She replaced negative thoughts with positive affirmations and encouraging statements. She reminded herself of her worth, strengths, and past achievements. Gradually, her self–talk became more compassionate, empowering, and supportive. As Ingrid practiced her new approach to self–talk, she noticed remarkable changes in her life. She felt a newfound sense of peace and contentment within herself. She embraced her flaws and imperfections with kindness, realising that they were part of her unique journey. This acceptance allowed her to let go of judgment and comparison, freeing her to fully embrace her authentic self. Also, Ingrid's relationships transformed as well. Her compassionate self–talk enabled her to approach interactions with empathy and understanding. She listened more attentively and communicated her thoughts and feelings more effectively. Her newfound clarity and authenticity deepened her connections and nurtured deeper and more meaningful relationships. Ingrid's story serves as a reminder that by changing your self–talk, you can cultivate a heart–led life filled with love, acceptance, and joy. Through her transformation, she discovered the profound impact of self–talk on her emotional well–being and relationships. Her story provides an example that by harnessing the power of your words, you can shape your thoughts, emotions, and ultimately, your lives.

**Reflective Exercise: Ingrid's Journey**

Here are four profound and reflective questions inspired by Ingrid's story to help you engage with your own neurolinguistic journey:

1. **How do you speak to yourself when no one is listening?** *Reflection:* Ingrid discovered that her private thoughts shaped her emotional world. You too carry an inner voice, sometimes kind, sometimes critical. Becoming aware of your internal dialogue is the first act of emotional courage. What if your self-talk could become your greatest ally, not your harshest critic?
2. **Where did your current patterns of self-talk originate, and are they still true?** *Reflection:* Many of Ingrid's beliefs were grounded in old conditioning and experiences that no longer served her. Your inner language might echo the voices of the past, but you have the power to rewrite the script. Begin by questioning whose words you are carrying, and whether they reflect the truth of your heart today.
3. **What would it feel like to speak to yourself with the same love and compassion you offer others?** *Reflection:* Ingrid could give love freely, yet struggled to turn that love inward. You may do the same, but when you soften toward yourself, the whole world softens with you. Self-kindness is not indulgence, it is the soil in which your courage, growth, and authenticity take root.
4. **How might your relationships change if your inner dialogue became more heart-led and empowering?** *Reflection:* Ingrid found that healing her self-talk brought depth and connection to her relationships. When you speak to yourself with honesty and love, your outer communication becomes clearer, more empathetic, and real. Every relationship you nurture begins with the one you have with yourself.

Let Ingrid's story remind you: words have power, and when spoken from the heart, even silently to yourself, they can become the most transformative medicine you carry.

**Affirmations For Integration: (Heart Whispers)**

Affirmations have the power to quiet the noise of doubt, open the doorway to self-trust, and draw you back into the wisdom of your heart. When practised daily, they nurture an inner dialogue based in love and truth, helping you live each day more aligned with who you truly are. I invite you to repeat silently or write:

- *I am rewiring my thoughts for positive change and empowered heart connection.*
- *I am using language to shape my reality.*
- *I am exploring the power of neurolinguistics to open a path with my heart.*
- *I am reprogramming my mind for success.*
- *I am harnessing the language of my mind to connect with my heart.*
- *I am choosing words that reflect love, truth, and possibility.*
- *I am transforming old patterns by speaking with clarity and compassion.*
- *I am aligning my language with the wisdom of my heart.*
- *I am creating a new story that empowers my growth and freedom.*

**"Voice of the Heart" Recording Exercise**

Your voice carries a unique resonance that your mind and body instinctively recognise as safe, familiar, and grounding. By recording yourself speaking words of kindness, affirmation, and compassion, you give yourself the gift of hearing your own heart reflected back to you, creating a powerful loop of self-love and healing.

1. **Create Your Script**: Write down 3–5 personal affirmations, compassionate truths, or heart-centred reminders. Examples might include:
    - *I am worthy of love just as I am.*
    - *Each day I grow in wisdom, strength, and compassion.*
    - *I choose to live with an open heart, even in moments of uncertainty.*
    - *My life is unfolding in alignment with a greater purpose.*

2. **Record with Intention**: Find a quiet space and record yourself reading your affirmations slowly and gently, as though speaking to someone you deeply care about. Speak from the heart. Let your tone carry warmth and sincerity.
3. **Listen Regularly**: Play your recording each morning upon waking and again each evening before sleep. Repetition helps reinforce positive neural and emotional pathways, gradually replacing old, critical inner voices with a voice of kindness and support.
4. **Notice the Shifts**: With time, your nervous system begins to associate your own voice with safety, encouragement, and trust. Instead of your inner dialogue defaulting to fear or criticism, you start to hear compassion, reassurance, and possibility.

This practice is not simply about affirmations, it is about reclaiming your voice as a tool of healing, teaching your heart and mind to work together, and building a daily ritual of self-connection. Over time, this becomes a sacred reminder: *you are your own source of strength, love, and guidance.*

**Closing Reflection**

The words you speak, especially the ones you whisper silently to yourself, hold extraordinary power. They are not fleeting sounds or passing thoughts, they are seeds. Every word takes root in the soil of your heart and mind, shaping the emotions you feel, directing the choices you make, and colouring the lens through which you experience your world. Neurolinguistics reminds you that language is more than a tool for communication, it is a vessel for transformation. When you speak with intention, when you reframe your thoughts with compassion, and when you anchor your inner dialogue in truth and hope, you are not simply changing your vocabulary, you are rewiring your brain, reshaping your inner reality, and realigning your life with possibility. Let this part of the journey remind you: each word you choose is a doorway. Some doors lead back to old fears and limitations, while others open into healing, clarity, and freedom. The choice is yours in every moment. Speak words that are kind, courageous, and heart-led. As you learn to listen to your inner dialogue with gentleness and curiosity, you discover that you are not only the listener but also the narrator, the author of your own unfolding story. You hold the pen. You hold the voice. You hold the power. May your words no longer confine you but instead liberate you. May they carry you closer to your truth, your wholeness, and your heart. Speak kindly. Speak consciously.

Speak as if every word is a step back home, because it is.

**Continue the Courage**

The courage you showed in reading this module deserves to grow. The Unbound journey offers more guidance, more breakthroughs, and more moments that remind you what you are capable of – www.timetotransform.world

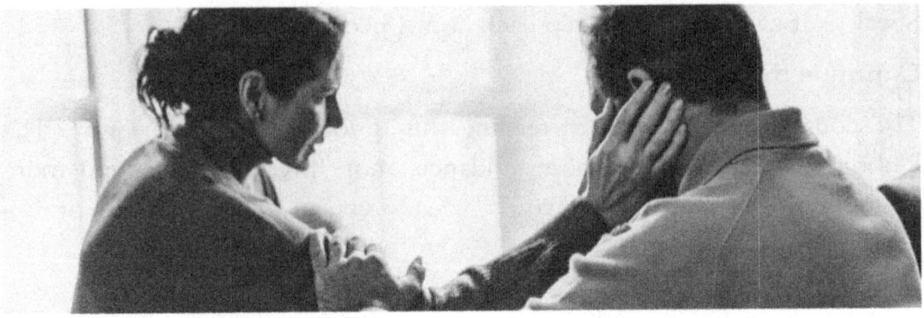

# MODULE 6 – COMPASSION

**Your Opening Reflection**

**Invitation to Compassion** - As you open this module, I invite you to place your hand over your heart and breathe gently into the space beneath your palm. Imagine compassion as a warm light, flowing first toward yourself, then radiating outward to others. This is your reminder that compassion is not weakness but strength, the courage to meet pain with tenderness, to hold yourself and others with kindness, and to soften instead of harden. Let this moment be your entry point into a deeper practice of living with an open heart..

- "Think of a time when you struggled. How would it have felt if someone had offered you kindness instead of judgment?"
- "What does compassion look like in action for you, toward yourself, toward others, or toward the world
- "When you witness suffering, big or small, what is your first instinct? To turn away, to fix it, or to connect with it?"
- "If compassion were a language, what words or gestures would you use to speak it more fluently in your everyday life?"
- "When was the last time someone showed you compassion? How did it make you feel?"
- "What would change in your life if you showed yourself the same compassion you offer others?"

Let these questions open the doorway into presence. Every answer you give, whether in words, sensations, or silence, is a bridge between where you are and where you are going.

### Learning Objectives

The learning objectives are included here to give you a clear focus for this module, ensuring that each practice you explore moves you closer to mastering the skills, insights, and heart-led awareness that will enrich your life well beyond the program. By the end of this module, you will:

- Understand the emotional and neurological benefits of practicing compassion.
- Develop skills in self-compassion, empathy, and compassionate communication.
- Explore the relationship between compassion and healing, connection, and leadership.
- Apply compassion in both personal and professional contexts to create positive change.

### Core Emotional Domains

The core emotional intelligence domains covered here are essential because they form the foundation for lasting heart connection, guiding you to deepen self-awareness, regulate emotions, build resilience, and strengthen the mind-body bond throughout your *Unbound* journey.

- **Self-Awareness:** invites you to recognise your own pain and humanity as the starting point for compassion.
- **Self-Regulation:** helps you respond rather than react, creating space to hold others' emotions without being overwhelmed.
- **Empathy:** deepens as you see beyond the surface and honour the shared experiences that unite us all.
- **Social Skills:** are enriched as compassion develops genuine connection, healing conflict, and strengthening trust.
- **Motivation:** becomes heart-aligned as your drive to act is fuelled by kindness, service, and the desire to uplift others.

### "Compassion – The Heart Of Connection"

Compassion is more than a kind gesture, it is a transformative force of emotional intelligence that elevates both personal well-being and collective humanity. At its core, compassion is the deep awareness of suffering, your own and others', combined with the heartfelt desire to relieve it. When turned inward, compassion becomes a powerful tool for healing. It helps you soften the inner critic, dissolve shame, and acknowledge your struggles without judgment. Instead of pushing yourself to 'get over it,' you learn to sit gently with your pain, to listen with tenderness, and to honour your human experience. This self-compassion builds true emotional resilience. It develops confidence not through perfection, but through kindness. When expressed outwardly, compassion becomes the bridge between people. It breaks down barriers of fear, anger, and misunderstanding. Compassionate communication allows for deeper listening, clearer understanding, and stronger, more authentic relationships. In high-performance environments like corporate settings, universities, or government departments, compassion enables more inclusive decision-making, reduces conflict, and fuels purpose-driven collaboration. Leaders who lead with compassion are not weak, they are strong enough to care. They are emotionally attuned to the needs of others, can hold space during conflict, and inspire trust and loyalty. Compassion transforms performance cultures into human-centred ones, where people are seen, heard, and valued. Compassion is not passive. It is active. It is not just a feeling, it is a conscious choice to be present, kind, and responsive, even when it is hard. It is the fuel for courageous conversations, the anchor during times of uncertainty, and the heartbeat of every act of service. In a world that is too often fractured by comparison, competition, and fear, compassion reminds you that you are not alone, and neither is anyone else. It invites you to be the one who listens deeper, who softens the edge, and who dares to care. This is how healing happens. This is how heart-led transformation begins.

## The History And Universality Of Compassion Across Cultures And Spiritual Traditions

Compassion is one of humanity's oldest and most revered virtues, an emotional and spiritual force that transcends time, geography, and belief systems. Across ancient civilisations and sacred traditions, compassion has been upheld as a path to both personal transformation and collective peace.

In **Buddhism**, compassion (karuṇā) is one of the Four Immeasurables, essential for liberation from suffering. It calls for active empathy and loving-kindness toward all beings. In **Christianity**, Jesus taught, *"Love your neighbour as yourself,"* embedding compassion at the heart of faith through parables, forgiveness, and service to the poor and vulnerable. **Islam** begins nearly every module of the Qur'an with *"In the name of God, the Most Compassionate, the Most Merciful,"* affirming rahmah (mercy) as a divine attribute to be lived by the faithful. **Hinduism** emphasises ahimsa, non-violence and compassion toward all living beings, as a foundational principle of spiritual life. **Judaism** teaches tikkun olam, or *"repairing the world,"* often through acts of compassion and justice. **Sikhism** speaks of daya, or compassionate sensitivity, as a vital expression of devotion to God and service to humanity.

In **Indigenous traditions** around the world, compassion is expressed through a deep kinship with all life, people, animals, the Earth, and ancestors. The sacred principle of reciprocity reminds us that care must flow in all directions for harmony to exist. Even in secular philosophy, from Confucian ethics to Stoic thought, compassion is seen as a key to ethical living and wise leadership. Modern psychology now echoes what ancient wisdom has always known: compassion is essential for mental health, community, and resilience. Despite differences in language, rituals, or belief, compassion remains a universal bridge, uniting hearts across continents, inviting people to rise above fear, and reminding you of your shared humanity. It is not bound to any one religion or culture. It is a sacred thread woven through them all, whispering the same truth: that to live fully is to love deeply, and to be truly human is to care.

## Compassion vs. Empathy: Understanding The Distinction And Synergy

Empathy and compassion are often used interchangeably, but they are distinct emotional capacities, each powerful on its own, and transformative when combined. **Empathy** is the ability to feel or understand what another person is experiencing. It comes in two primary forms:

- **Emotional empathy**: where you actually *feel* another's emotions, as if they were your own.
- **Cognitive empathy**: where you intellectually *understand* what someone is feeling, even if you do not feel it yourself.

Empathy allows you to tune in, to walk in another's shoes, and to resonate with their internal world, but without boundaries or action, empathy alone can lead to **empathic distress,** an emotional overload that can result in burnout, especially in caring professions or high-stress environments. **Compassion**, on the other hand, takes empathy a step further. It adds two crucial ingredients: **a desire to alleviate suffering** and **a conscious choice**

**to act with care**. Compassion is empathy in motion. It includes warmth, perspective, and intentional response. Where empathy feels *with*, compassion feels *for*, and *moves toward*. The **synergy** between them is profound. Empathy creates the connection. Compassion channels it into wise, heartful action. In emotionally intelligent relationships, workplaces, and leadership, this blend creates not only mutual understanding but also resilience, inclusion, and trust. In short:

- **Empathy says**: *"I feel what you are feeling."*
- **Compassion says**: *"I see your pain, and I want to help ease it."*

When you learn to navigate both, empathising without being overwhelmed, and responding with compassionate intention, you open the door to deeper connection, sustainable caregiving, and a more heart-led way of being.

**The Science Of Compassion: Effects On The Brain, Body, And Emotional Wellbeing**

Compassion is not only a spiritual virtue or moral ideal, it is a **biological capacity** wired into your human system. Thanks to advances in neuroscience, Compassion is not only a spiritual virtue or moral ideal, it is a **biological capacity** wired into your human system. Thanks to advances in neuroscience, psychology, and mind-body medicine, we now know that compassion has **measurable, transformative effects** on your brain, body, and emotional health.

<u>Compassion and the Brain: Rewiring for Connection</u>

Compassion activates specific regions of your brain associated with empathy, reward, and emotional regulation:

- Your **anterior cingulate cortex** and **insula** light up during compassionate responses, facilitating emotional awareness and motivation to help.
- The **ventral striatum,** a key part of your brain's reward system, is activated when you act with compassion, reinforcing pro-social behavior with a sense of pleasure or satisfaction.
- The **prefrontal cortex**, responsible for your executive function and impulse control, is strengthened by compassion meditation, enhancing emotional regulation and mindful decision-making.

Repeated acts of compassion, even imagined or intentional ones, **retrain**

**neural pathways** toward care, presence, and connection. Through a process called **neuroplasticity**, your brain literally reshapes itself to become more compassionate over time.

Compassion and the Body: Healing Through Heartfulness

Biologically, compassion enables a shift from stress to safety. When you act compassionately, whether toward yourself or others, your body enters a state of calm and repair:

- **Oxytocin**, known as the *"bonding hormone,"* is released, increasing trust and lowering blood pressure.
- **Heart rate variability (HRV)** improves, a sign of emotional resilience and nervous system balance.
- **Cortisol**, the body's stress hormone, decreases significantly during compassionate states.
- The **immune system** strengthens, as chronic inflammation, the root of many illnesses, is reduced.
- Compassion literally **heals your body**, reinforcing the link between emotional connection and physical vitality.
- Participants in **Compassion Cultivation Training (CCT)** reported greater empathy, reduced emotional reactivity, and enhanced wellbeing in as little as 8 weeks.

These findings offer hope: no matter your starting point, **you can become more compassionate**, toward yourself and others.

The Takeaway

Compassion is not weakness; it is your greatest neurobiological strength. When you allow yourself to meet your pain or another's suffering with kindness, you activate powerful systems in your brain and nervous system that restore balance, safety, and healing. Compassion is not indulgence; it is a force that reconditions your mind and soothes your heart. It is not optional; it is essential, for your health, your heart, and your humanity. Each time you choose compassion, you are teaching your body to soften stress, your mind to let go of fear, and your soul to remember what matters most. In a world that often demands performance, perfection, and pressure, compassion becomes your quiet revolution. It rewires your nervous system, strengthens your resilience, and awakens your courage. It shows you that love is not only an emotion but also the most intelligent response you can make. When you embody compassion, you step into alignment with the truth of your heart. You liberate yourself from judgment and create space for connection, healing, and peace, within yourself and in the world around you.

### Compassion As A Leadership Quality And Driver Of Emotional Maturity

In the evolving landscape of leadership, compassion is no longer viewed as a soft or optional trait, it is a core competency for effective, emotionally intelligent leaders and a catalyst for meaningful human connection, organisational wellbeing, and sustained performance.

#### Compassionate Leadership: Leading with Heart and Strength

True leadership is not just about authority or vision, it is about presence, relational intelligence, and trust. Compassionate leaders:

- **See the person, not just the role**. You recognise the humanity behind the job title, and respond with empathy when others are struggling.
- **Listen deeply** and respond with care, not to fix, but to understand and empower.
- **Model psychological safety**, allowing others to be vulnerable, take creative risks, and speak their truth without fear of judgement.
- **Balance accountability with empathy**, knowing that high performance grows best in a culture of respect and care.

Far from making leaders appear weak, compassion earns respect, builds loyalty, and creates environments where people want to give their best.

#### Compassion as a Sign of Emotional Maturity

Compassion is emotional intelligence in action. It draws on and strengthens key EI domains:

- **Self-awareness**: Compassion requires you to notice your internal reactions, judgement, impatience, or defensiveness, and pause before responding.
- **Self-regulation**: Rather than reacting harshly, you choose a response that supports growth, for yourself and others.
- **Empathy**: You actively imagine what it feels like to be in someone else's shoes, without needing to agree or fix.

- **Motivation**: Compassionate leaders are motivated by a desire to serve a purpose greater than themselves.
- **Social skills**: Compassion deepens your ability to manage relationships, navigate conflict, and inspire teams.

Choosing compassion, especially in difficult moments, is a sign of **emotional strength**, not softness. It reflects maturity, humility, and wisdom. Compassion is not only a spiritual virtue or moral ideal, it is a **biological capacity** wired into your human system. Thanks to advances in neuroscience, Compassion is not only a spiritual virtue or moral ideal, it is a **biological capacity** wired into your human system. Thanks to advances in neuroscience, psychology, and mind-body medicine, we now know that compassion has **measurable, transformative effects** on your brain, body, and emotional health.

**Compassion And The Brain: Rewiring For Connection**

Compassion activates specific regions of your brain associated with empathy, reward, and emotional regulation:

- Your **anterior cingulate cortex** and **insula** light up during compassionate responses, facilitating emotional awareness and motivation to help.
- The **ventral striatúm,** a key part of your brain's reward system, is activated when you act with compassion, reinforcing pro-social behavior with a sense of pleasure or satisfaction.
- The **prefrontal cortex**, responsible for your executive function and impulse control, is strengthened by compassion meditation, enhancing emotional regulation and mindful decision-making.

Repeated acts of compassion, even imagined or intentional ones, **retrain neural pathways** toward care, presence, and connection. Through a process called **neuroplasticity**, your brain literally reshapes itself to become more compassionate over time.

**Why Self-Compassion Is The Foundation Of True Compassion For Others**

You cannot pour from an empty cup, and in the realm of emotional intelligence, this truth becomes even more profound. Self-compassion is not self-indulgence or weakness. It is the very foundation upon which authentic compassion for others is built.

You Cannot Give What You Do Not Have

When you are harsh with yourself, judging, criticising, or berating your mistakes, it becomes harder to offer genuine understanding to others. Why? Because unacknowledged inner pain often leads to projection, burnout, or emotional distance. Self-compassion softens your inner world. It teaches you to:

- Embrace imperfection as part of being human.
- Respond to your struggles with kindness, not condemnation.
- Honour your needs and emotional landscape without guilt.

In doing so, you create space, emotional spaciousness, to meet others with the same grace.

Compassion Begins in the Mirror

People often assume compassion is outward-focused, but it starts within. When you treat yourself with warmth, patience, and understanding, you rewire your nervous system for safety and trust. You stop seeing others through a lens of comparison, competition, or judgement, and instead view them through a shared humanity. Self-compassion allows you to say:

- *"Just like me, they make mistakes."*
- *"Just like me, they are trying."*
- *"Just like me, they long to be seen and loved."*

This recognition dismantles barriers. It dissolves *"otherness."* It makes empathy more than a thought, it makes it embodied.

The Science of Self-Compassion

Research by Dr. Kristin Neff and others has shown that self-compassion:

- Activates the parasympathetic nervous system (calm, grounded state).
- Lowers cortisol and reduces chronic stress.
- Builds resilience and emotional regulation.
- Enhances motivation, not through fear, but through inner support.

People who practice self-compassion are more likely to:

- Offer help to others without resentment or martyrdom.

- Apologise and repair relationships.
- Maintain healthy boundaries.
- Act with courage, even after failure.

Self-Compassion Cultivates Emotional Generosity

When you are kind to yourself, your compassion becomes more spacious. You are less likely to take things personally, react from pain, or withdraw when others struggle. Instead, you offer presence. Understanding. A heart that says, "*I have been there too. I see you.*" In this way, self-compassion does not limit your compassion, it **amplifies** it.

**Compassion-in-Action Toolkit**

This week, I invite you to choose *at least two* of the following acts of compassion. Each small action you take has the power to ripple outward, nurturing your own heart while touching the lives of others.

1. **Self-compassion ritual** – Write a compassionate affirmation just for you and place it near your mirror. Each morning when you see it, pause, breathe, and let those words settle into your heart.
2. **Active listening moment** – In your next conversation, give the gift of your full presence. Put away distractions, soften your attention, and truly listen, not just to the words spoken, but to the feelings behind them.
3. **Forgiveness practice** – Reflect on one burden you have been carrying, a hurt, a resentment, a grudge. Write a letter of forgiveness, not to condone or excuse, but to release your own heart from its weight. You do not need to send it; the act of writing is enough.
4. **Service contribution** – Offer one hour of your time this week to help someone without expectation. It could be assisting a colleague, supporting a friend, or volunteering in your community. Let your service be an expression of love without condition.
5. **Kindness ripple** – Choose a simple, anonymous act of kindness. It could be leaving a kind note, paying for someone's coffee, or sending encouragement without signing your name. Trust that your gesture, though unseen, will brighten someone's day.

### Case Study Discussion: Grace's Journey

Grace was a 42 year–old woman who had always lived a fairly self–centred and disconnected life. By her own admission she was consumed by her own desires and needs, rarely considering the feelings and struggles of others. During one of our sessions, she told me about a series of events that led her to question the way she had been living and about a chance encounter where she witnessed an act of kindness between strangers. It was only a small thing in the overall scheme of life, but she told me that she had seen a man offer his coat to a homeless woman on a cold winter night. The compassion displayed in that moment struck a chord deep within her heart. It was a wake-up call that made her realise the emptiness of her own existence. Grace was inspired by this encounter, and she embarked on a powerful journey of self–reflection and transformation. She started by practicing self–compassion, learning to be kind, and forgiving towards herself. As she extended this compassion to herself, she discovered a newfound sense of peace and acceptance. In time, Grace began to extend her compassion to others. It was difficult for her at the start, but she volunteered at a local charity store, offering her time and support to those in need. She spent time and listened to their stories, held their hands, and offered words of encouragement. In each act of compassion, she experienced a deep connection with others and a profound sense of purpose. As Grace continued on her path of compassion, she encountered profound changes in her life. Relationships that were once strained (especially with her parents) started to heal as she approached them with understanding and empathy. She also became a trusted confidante and a source of comfort for her friends and family. In her professional life, Grace's newfound compassion transformed the dynamics of her team. She became a source of inspiration, encouraging her workmates to work together and support one another. Outside of her immediate circle, Grace found herself drawn to causes that championed social justice and equality. In time she became an advocate for homeless teenagers in her area, using her voice to raise awareness and bring about change. Her acts of compassion extended beyond individuals, encompassing the broader community. Through her journey of embracing compassion, Grace experienced a profound shift in her life. The once self–centred woman that I had first encountered had evolved into a beautiful beacon of light and love. Her heart overflowed with kindness, and she radiated a warmth that touched the lives of those around her and she was a joy to be around. In the process of embracing compassion, Grace discovered the true essence of her being. She realised that life's true purpose was about connecting with others, offering support, and showing kindness. It was through compassion that she found fulfillment, joy, and a profound sense of belonging. Grace's story is a testament to the transformative power of compassion. It demonstrates that when you choose to open your heart to others and embrace empathy and kindness, you not only transform your own life but also create a ripple effect of positive change in those around you.

**Reflective Exercise: Grace's Journey**

Here are two profound and reflective questions inspired by Grace's story to help you engage with your own compassionate journey:

1. **When was the last time you offered yourself compassion instead of criticism?** *Supportive Reflection:* Just like Grace, your journey begins with how you treat yourself. Your inner voice matters. Are you offering yourself the same kindness and patience you give to others? When you make a mistake or feel overwhelmed, could you try saying to yourself, "I'm doing the best I can, and that's enough"?
2. **How might you see the humanity in others more clearly today, even those who challenge you?** *Supportive Reflection:* That simple moment Grace witnessed, a man offering his coat, reminds you that small acts of kindness can awaken deep truths. Every person you encounter is carrying invisible struggles. When you choose to meet them with curiosity and compassion, you open the door to deeper connection and healing.

**Affirmations For Integration: (Heart Whispers)**

Affirmations have the power to quiet the noise of doubt, open the doorway to self-trust, and draw you back into the wisdom of your heart. When practised daily, they nurture an inner dialogue based in love and truth, helping you live each day more aligned with who you truly are. I invite you to repeat silently or write:

- *I choose to show compassion to people in my life.*
- *I am committed to doing acts of kindness for others.*
- *I open my heart to the pain and struggles of others.*

- *I embrace forgiveness to embrace compassion and healing.*
- *I strive to listen deeply and validate the experiences of others.*
- *I believe in the power of compassion to create positive change in the world.*

**Compassion Reflection Exercise**

Take a 30-minute walk with the clear intention of awakening your heart to compassion. As you step outside, allow yourself to slow down and notice the people passing by, the rhythms of nature, the quiet details of your surroundings. With each step, ask yourself:

- *Where is compassion needed here?*
- *Where can I offer kindness, within me and around me?*

If you see someone rushing, instead of judging, breathe in patience. If you notice an elderly person or a child, silently bless them with safety and love. If you witness tension, offer an inward prayer for peace. If you pass by a tree, flower, or bird, acknowledge the gift of life it holds and the interconnectedness you share.

As you walk, extend compassion inward too. Notice if self-criticism or restlessness arises, and gently replace it with kindness toward yourself. Let your heart guide your gaze, your breath, and your thoughts. When you return, take a few moments to journal. Write down what you noticed, how the walk made you feel, and whether compassion shifted the way you saw the world. Ask yourself:

- *What action am I called to take now, from this heart-awakened place?*

This walk is not just an exercise, it is a living practice, training your mind and heart to choose compassion as your natural way of seeing.

## Closing Reflection

Compassion is not something you simply give away, it is a force that reshapes you from within. Every time you choose compassion, whether toward yourself or others, you send ripples through your nervous system, calming fear and dissolving judgment. You rewire your brain for connection rather than separation, for healing rather than harm. Remember: compassion is not weakness, it is courage. It is not indulgence, it is intelligence. It is not optional, it is essential, for your heart, your health, and your humanity. As you walk this path, let compassion become both your anchor and your compass.

Notice how it changes your inner dialogue, softens your relationships, and expands your presence in the world. When pressure rises, return to compassion. When criticism echoes, return to compassion. When the world feels heavy, return to compassion. In doing so, you are not only offering love to others, you are offering love to yourself, and in that simple, profound choice, you awaken the quiet revolution of the heart.

### Transformation Loves Momentum

Do not stop now. Momentum is a sacred energy, once it moves, let it carry you. Another Unbound chapter, book, or online experience will help you keep that energy alive – **www.timetotransform.world**

# MODULE 7– LISTENING

**Your Opening Reflection**

**Invitation to Listen Deeply -** As you enter this module I invite you to experience listening as more than hearing words, as an act of love. True listening is presence: to another person, to the world around you, and to your own heart. It asks nothing but your attention, your stillness, your willingness to receive without judgment. Each time you listen with openness, you give someone, or yourself, the gift of feeling valued, seen, and safe. Let this module be your reminder that listening is not passive; it is one of the most powerful ways to connect, to heal, and to honour what matters most.

- "When was the last time you felt truly heard?"
- "How did that moment impact you emotionally?"
- "When you listen to others, do you truly hear their words, or are you waiting for your turn to respond?"
- "What does it feel like in your body when someone listens to you with full presence and no judgment?"
- "How do you listen to your own inner voice, do you give it space, or do you silence it?"
- "In what relationships would deeper listening create more connection, healing, or trust?"

Let these questions open the doorway into presence. Every answer you give, whether in words, sensations, or silence, is a bridge between where you are and where you are going.

## Learning Objectives

The learning objectives are included here to give you a clear focus for this module, ensuring that each practice you explore moves you closer to mastering the skills, insights, and heart-led awareness that will enrich your life well beyond the program. By the end of this module, you will:

- Understand the emotional intelligence behind active, empathetic, and reflective listening
- Explore how deep listening nurtures trust, compassion, and relational safety
- Practise techniques to enhance personal and interpersonal listening skills
- Recognise the role of silence and stillness in accessing heart wisdom

## Core Emotional Domains

The core emotional intelligence domains covered here are essential because they form the foundation for lasting heart connection, guiding you to deepen self-awareness, regulate emotions, build resilience, and strengthen the mind-body bond throughout your *Unbound* journey.

- **Self-Awareness:** Listening opens a window into your inner world. You begin to notice your urge to interrupt, your emotional triggers, and your habitual patterns. As you listen more deeply, you hear not only others, but yourself.
- **Social Awareness (Empathy):** True listening asks you to step into someone else's experience. You tune into tone, body language, and what's left unsaid. In that stillness, empathy awakens. You connect not to fix, but to feel.
- **Relationship Management:** Listening is the foundation of connection. It builds trust, de-escalates conflict, and invites honest conversation. Through active, heart-led listening, you create space where others feel seen, heard, and valued.
- **Emotional Regulation:** To truly listen, you learn to regulate your own emotions. You pause, breathe, and stay present even when the conversation is hard. In that pause, you choose compassion over reaction.

- **Communication & Interpersonal Effectiveness:** Listening refines your communication. You respond with intention, not impulse. You speak less, but with more meaning. Your relationships deepen, not because you say more, but because you hear with your heart.

**"Listening - The Art Of Deep Connection"**

When you truly listen, with your whole heart, not just your ears, you invite a deeper level of understanding and compassion into your life. Listening asks more of you than simply staying quiet. It asks you to *be present.* To place your full attention in the moment. To resist the urge to judge, to fix, or to interrupt. When you listen deeply to someone else, you are saying: *"You matter. I care about what you feel. I am here with you."* That level of presence can soften conflict, dissolve misunderstanding, and build trust that words alone cannot reach, but perhaps even more important than listening to others… is learning how to listen to yourself. You have spent so much time in the noise of the world, external expectations, endless demands, self-criticism. It is easy to forget that beneath all of that, your heart is still speaking. Are you listening? When you take time to pause… to breathe… to slow your thoughts and drop into your body… you begin to hear that inner voice. The one that knows what you need. The one that remembers who you are. That voice may have been silenced, dismissed, or ignored in the past, but it never left you. It is still there, waiting patiently to be heard. Listening to your heart is one of the most profound acts of self-respect you can offer. It is how you begin to align with your truth. It is how you know when to say yes, when to say no, and when to choose stillness instead of reaction. Through this part of your *Unbound* journey, you are invited to become a listener, not just in conversation, but in life. To listen to the unspoken stories beneath someone's words. To hear the emotions behind the silence, and to attune to your own inner world with curiosity, kindness, and presence. Listening changes everything. It deepens connection. It builds empathy, and most of all, it creates space for healing, within you, and between you and the world.

**The Difference Between Hearing And Heart-Based Listening**

There is a world of difference between *hearing* someone and *truly listening* to them with your heart. You hear with your ears, but you listen with your whole being. Hearing is passive. It happens automatically. Sounds come in, words are registered, and you may even nod or reply, but in this state, you are often distracted, rehearsing your response, or filtering what is said through your own assumptions and beliefs.

Heart-based listening is something altogether different.

Heart-based listening is something altogether different. When you engage in heart-based listening, you offer more than your ears, you offer your full presence. You quiet the noise of your mind, soften the pull of distraction, and step aside from the urge to fix, advise, or prove yourself right. Instead, you lean into stillness and allow yourself to simply be with the person before you. In this space, you do not just hear words; you feel the person, their tone, their pauses, their energy, their unspoken emotions. You sense the intention beneath their expression, the longing beneath their story. Your heart becomes a mirror, reflecting back not judgment but understanding, not correction but compassion. Through heart-based listening, you create a sanctuary where another person feels safe enough to bring their whole self. They feel valued not for perfect phrasing or polished expression, but for their truth, raw and real. To listen in this way is to say without words: *"You matter. Your voice matters. Your being matters."* This kind of listening transforms conversations into connection, and connection into healing.

Heart-based listening is the gateway to healing.

When you listen this way, you open the door to deep connection. You build bridges where walls once stood. You learn to pause before reacting, to seek understanding before judgement, and to communicate from a place of compassion rather than defensiveness, and this same principle applies when you turn inward. You may have spent years *hearing* your inner voice, your doubts, your fears, your needs, but brushing them aside. Dismissing them with logic or burying them beneath busyness, but when you listen from your heart, you begin to honour that inner voice with the same love and care you give to others. Heart-based listening is not always easy. It asks you to be vulnerable. To slow down. To face what is really being said, by others and by yourself, but in doing so, you become someone who truly hears. Someone who listens for the *meaning*, the *emotion*, and the *heart* behind the message, and that kind of listening transforms relationships. It transforms your relationship with yourself, and ultimately, it transforms your life.

**The Science And Psychology Of Active Listening (Carl Rogers, Socratic Dialogue)**

Active listening is not just a soft skill, it is a profound psychological and emotional practice grounded in evidence-based science and centuries of human wisdom. When you listen actively, you do not just absorb someone's words, you become a vessel for understanding, empathy, and transformation. At the heart of this practice lies the work of renowned psychologist **Carl Rogers**, who believed that *unconditional positive regard*, *empathic understanding*, and *congruence* were essential conditions for personal growth and healing. Rogers did not see listening as something you do with your ears alone, he taught that real listening means tuning into the emotional frequency of the speaker with your whole heart. When you listen through the lens of **Rogersian psychology**, you offer the other person a rare and sacred gift: the space to be truly seen, without judgment. You withhold advice. You refrain from interrupting. You listen not to reply, but to understand, and through that presence, healing occurs, often without a single solution being offered. Even earlier in history, the **Socratic method** demonstrated another dimension of listening: *the art of asking meaningful, clarifying questions.* Socrates believed that truth and wisdom emerge not from telling others what to think, but from listening closely and helping them uncover their own insights through open, reflective dialogue. This is also the essence of heart-based listening in *The Unbound Lawyer* program. You are not listening to win. You are not listening to fix. You are listening to *connect.*

From a **neuroscientific perspective**, active listening activates areas of the brain associated with empathy and compassion, such as the anterior insula and the mirror neuron system. It soothes your amygdala's fight-or-flight response, builds trust, and co-regulates emotional states in both speaker and listener. In fact, research shows that feeling heard and understood reduces cortisol (the stress hormone), improves immune function, and boosts oxytocin, your bonding hormone. When you engage in true, intentional listening, you help the other person feel safe, and safety is the foundation of all authentic relationship. Listening in this way requires *self-regulation*, *self-awareness*, and *emotional maturity*. It is a discipline and a devotion, to yourself and to others. It invites you to become not just a passive receiver of sound, but an *active witness to someone's inner world, a*nd when you offer this gift of presence, you invite others to do the same for you.

**Barriers To Effective Listening: Judgment, Inner Chatter, Impatience**

True listening is a profound act of presence, but it is not always easy. While your heart may long to understand and connect, there are often silent saboteurs that stand in the way. These barriers, judgment, inner chatter, and impatience, are subtle but powerful, and they can disconnect you from others and from your own deeper wisdom.

Judgment: The Wall That Silences Connection

Judgment is one of the most common and insidious barriers to listening. It is the voice inside you that decides who is right, who is wrong, who is worthy, and who is not, even before the other person has finished speaking. When you judge, you filter what you hear through assumptions, labels, and past experiences. Instead of receiving someone's words openly, you interpret them through a narrow lens. You stop listening with your heart and start listening with your opinions. This prevents real connection and can make others feel unsafe or unseen. To overcome this, you must practice *suspending judgment.* It does not mean agreeing with everything, it means staying open long enough to *understand* before you assess. It means choosing curiosity over criticism, compassion over conclusion.

Inner Chatter: The Noise Within

Even when you are quiet on the outside, there is often a whirlwind on the inside, planning your response, remembering your own story, or drifting to your to-do list. This is your *inner chatter,* the mental noise that keeps you from being fully present. When your attention is split between listening and your own internal dialogue, you miss the subtle cues, the emotional undertones, and the deeper meaning of what is being shared. You hear the words, but not the heart behind them. To quiet the inner chatter, return to your breath. Anchor yourself in the moment. Repeat inwardly, *"I am here. I am listening."* Let the speaker's words be the only voice you follow for that moment. This is heart-based listening, offering your full attention as a sacred gift.

Impatience: The Urge to Fix, Finish, or Flee

In a world conditioned for speed and solutions, *impatience* often shows up in your listening. You might interrupt. You might rush someone to the point. You might mentally check out because you feel like you "*already know where this is going,*" but effective listening requires *patience.* People need space to find their words, feel their way through their thoughts, and speak from their hearts. If you rush that process, you risk cutting off something vulnerable, meaningful, or healing. Impatience often masks your own discomfort, your desire to control, to move on, or to be *"right,"* but heart-based listening invites you to *slow down* and *stay.* It teaches you that healing often comes not from advice or answers, but from feeling heard in the presence of loving stillness. When you become aware of these barriers, judgment, inner chatter, and impatience, you take a powerful step toward more conscious, compassionate connection. You learn to listen not just with your ears, but with your *whole self,* and in doing so, you open the door to healing, both for yourself and for those you love.

**The Impact Of Listening On Emotional Safety And Trust In Relationships**

Listening is more than a skill, it is a sacred act of love. When you truly listen to someone, with your heart open and your presence undivided, you do something extraordinary: you create emotional safety. You become a sanctuary, and in that space of safety, trust is born. Emotional safety is the foundation of all healthy relationships, whether with a partner, a child, a friend, a colleague, or yourself. It is the felt sense of being seen, heard, valued, and accepted without fear of judgment, interruption, or rejection, and the fastest way to build that safety is through deep, intentional listening.

<u>When You Listen, You Tell Someone They Matter</u>

Think about the last time someone truly listened to you. Not just nodded along. Not just waited for their turn to speak, but really *listened,* with full presence, empathy, and a desire to understand. *How did it make you feel?* Chances are, you felt more than just heard. You felt *affirmed.* You felt like your feelings were valid. You felt like *you mattered.* This is the power of heart-based listening, it affirms worthiness and creates belonging. In a world that moves quickly and often superficially, this kind of listening is revolutionary.

<u>Listening as a Bridge Between Hearts</u>

When you offer someone your listening presence, you open a bridge between your heart and theirs. You allow them to lower their defences. You signal, *"You are safe here."* That sense of safety allows vulnerability to unfold, and vulnerability is the birthplace of intimacy, healing, and growth. In couples, it renews connection. In friendships, it deepens authenticity. In teams and workplaces, it cultivates respect and collaboration. Conversely, when someone feels unheard, dismissed, or interrupted, emotional walls rise. Defensiveness appears. Trust withers, and disconnection grows. Listening is not just about gathering information, it is about *building relationship.* Every time you choose to listen with love instead of react with ego, you strengthen the emotional fabric that holds your relationships together.

Becoming a Safe Space, For Others and For Yourself

Heart-based listening also teaches you how to be safe with *yourself*. When you practice truly listening to your own emotions, without judgment, avoidance, or harshness, you begin to build inner trust. You tell yourself, *"My feelings matter. My inner voice deserves to be heard."* As that inner trust grows, so does your ability to listen to others with compassion. Your heart becomes more spacious, more patient, more attuned, and from this place, relationships flourish, not through perfection, but through presence. In *The Unbound Lawyer*, learning to listen with your whole heart is one of the most powerful gifts you can offer, to others, and to your own soul. It requires practice, patience, and humility, but the rewards are profound: deeper connection, emotional safety, and unshakeable trust.

**Listening To Self: Stillness, Intuition, And Inner Guidance**

In a world filled with noise, deadlines, opinions, and expectations, learning to listen to your *own voice* can feel like a radical act, but it is also one of the most essential steps on the path to heart connection. When you slow down and listen inwardly, with intention, with compassion, and with curiosity, you begin to hear what truly matters: your own inner guidance.

Stillness: The Gateway to Inner Listening

Stillness is not simply the absence of sound or movement, it is the presence of awareness. It is the sacred pause where your breath softens, your mind quiets, and your heart becomes audible. When you enter stillness, you are not escaping life, you are returning to yourself. It is in the quiet moments, free from distraction or urgency, that your heart begins to whisper the truths you have been too busy to hear. Sometimes, these whispers come as insights. Other times, they come as sensations in your body, or memories rising to the surface. Stillness is the space where listening becomes possible.

Intuition: The Language of the Heart

Your intuition is not a fantasy or a mystical anomaly, it is a natural, inner compass. It is the felt sense that guides you toward truth, alignment, and integrity, and it speaks in subtleties: a gut feeling, a quiet knowing, a gentle pull in a certain direction. When you take time to listen inwardly, you begin to strengthen your connection to this deep inner wisdom. You learn to differentiate between the noise of fear and the voice of clarity. You learn to honour what *feels right*, not just what *looks right* on paper. This is the language of the heart, and when you listen to it, your choices begin to reflect who you really are.

Inner Guidance: Reclaiming Trust in Yourself

Many of us have been conditioned to look outward for answers, to seek validation, advice, or approval from others. While there is value in wise counsel, there is a deeper wisdom that resides within you. You are not empty. You are not lost. You are not without direction. You have within you a wellspring of insight, discernment, and strength. Listening to yourself is an act of reclaiming trust. As you journey through *The Unbound Lawyer*, you are invited to tune in, not tune out. To ask your heart what it needs. To breathe into your body and feel what is alive. To write freely without censoring. To move when stillness becomes emotion. To rest when your soul asks for it. These are not small things, they are profound declarations that your inner world matters. When you listen to yourself with kindness and presence, you begin to live a life that is not just reactive, but *responsive*, aligned, and deeply attuned. You create space for inner peace, intuitive decisions, and the steady guidance of your own heart, and from that place, everything changes, not because the world is different, but because *you are.*

**"Empathy in Silence" (Paired Activity)**

This activity is designed to help you experience the power of listening without words, a practice of presence, patience, and heart connection.

1. **Pair Up** – Find a partner and decide who will share first.
2. **Share (2 minutes each)** – One participant shares something personal, it could be a story, a challenge, a joy, or simply how you are feeling in this moment. The other participant listens silently. There are **no interruptions, no advice, no fixing**. Your only task is to *be fully present.* Use eye contact, gentle nods, and soft facial expressions as subtle signals of support.
3. **Switch Roles** – After 2 minutes, change roles so each person has the opportunity to both share and listen.
4. **Silent Reflection (1 minute each)** – Before speaking again, both partners sit quietly for a short pause, noticing what they felt while listening and being listened to.
5. **Debrief Together** – Reflect with your partner:
   - What did it feel like to be listened to without interruption?

- What emotions surfaced as you held silent space for someone else?
- Did you notice the difference between listening with your head versus listening with your heart?

This exercise often reveals how rare it is to be heard without distraction or judgment. It teaches you that empathy is not always expressed in words, sometimes it is the stillness of your presence, the openness of your heart, and the safety of your silence that speak the loudest.

**Case Study Discussion: Daniel's Journey**

Daniel was really talkative, he loved sharing his ideas, thoughts, and experiences, but he rarely took the time to truly listen. He would often interrupt me in our sessions, and I would let him say his peace. I asked him why he was always on transmit, and how did that truly make him feel? Daniel told me that he found himself in a place where he felt disconnected and unsatisfied with his relationships and his life in general. In our sessions he realised that his inability to (actively) listen was a significant barrier to building meaningful connections and understanding others on a deeper level. He did it as a self–protective mechanism, but it came at a cost, and Daniel desperately wanted to transform his life. Daniel started by practicing active listening. He made a conscious effort to be fully present when someone was speaking to him, focusing on their words, body language, and emotions. I used to enjoy Daniel telling me how hard it was for him to resist the urge to interrupt and instead allow another person the opportunity to express themselves. What was interesting was that over time Daniel began to listen more attentively and he discovered the power of empathy. He realised that by truly listening, he could understand and connect with others on a deeper level (including himself).

Daniel started to ask open–ended questions and show genuine interest in their experiences, which nurtured stronger and more meaningful connections, friendships, and relationships. He also learned to appreciate silence and the spaces between words. He realised that sometimes, the most profound messages are conveyed through nonverbal cues and the unspoken. As Daniel practiced listening, he noticed a positive shift in his relationships. People felt valued and heard in his presence, and he created an environment where he learnt how to trust again. His newfound ability to listen deeply allowed for more open and honest communication, resolving conflicts, and nurturing harmony. Most importantly, Daniel discovered that by learning to listen, he found a greater sense of happiness and fulfillment in his own life. He realised that true listening is an act of love and compassion, and it allowed him to connect with himself on a deeper heart level. Through listening, he cultivated deeper relationships, gained new perspectives, and nurtured a sense of belonging and understanding. In the end, Daniel's journey of learning to listen transformed not only his relationships but also his own inner world. He became a better friend, partner, and listener, embracing the power of listening as a gateway to happiness and a more authentic and meaningful life.

**Reflective Exercise: Daniel's Journey**

Here are four profound and reflective questions inspired by Daniels story to help you engage with your own listening journey:

1. **When was the last time you truly listened, to yourself, without judgment, distraction, or the need to fix anything?** What did you hear in the stillness? What did your heart try to tell you when you finally gave it space to speak?
2. **Do you notice the difference between hearing someone's words and truly receiving their heart?** What barriers within you, like impatience, assumptions, or inner noise, get in the way of offering someone your full, present attention?
3. **What would change in your life if you listened more deeply, to your body's signals, your inner voice, your quiet truths?** How might your relationships, decisions, and sense of self evolve if you trusted what you feel as much as what you think?
4. **Who in your life needs to feel heard, not just with your ears, but with your presence and empathy?** How might you create emotional safety and deepen connection simply by offering your undivided, heart-based listening?

**Affirmations For You – (Heart Whispers)**

Affirmations have the power to quiet the noise of doubt, open the doorway to self-trust, and draw you back into the wisdom of your heart. When practised daily, they nurture an inner dialogue based in love and truth, helping you live each day more aligned with who you truly are. I invite you to repeat silently or write:

- *I give my full attention when someone is speaking to me.*
- *I listen with an open heart and an open mind.*
- *I seek to understand before being understood.*
- *I honour and respect the opinions and viewpoints of others.*
- *I embrace silence as an opportunity to listen deeply.*
- *I am curious and eager to learn from others' experiences.*
- *I create a safe space where others feel valued, seen, and heard.*

**Create a Listening Oath**

I invite you to write a personal **"Listening Commitment"** to yourself and those you care about. This is not just a set of promises, it is a declaration of the kind of presence you wish to bring into your relationships, your conversations, and your inner life. When you write your Oath, imagine it as a gentle compass that guides you back whenever you drift into distraction, impatience, or self-judgment.

Your Oath could include pledges such as:

- *"I will pause before responding, allowing space for others to finish and for me to reflect."*
- *"I will give eye contact and put away distractions, offering my full attention."*
- *"I will ask open-hearted questions that invite depth rather than quick answers."*
- *"I will listen to myself with kindness, honouring my own needs and emotions as I do others'."*
- *"I will hold silence as part of listening, trusting that words are not always necessary."*
- *"I will respect the courage it takes for others to share, even when their truth differs from mine."*

Once you have written your Oath, **display it somewhere visible,** perhaps in your journal, on your desk, or even as a note on your phone. You may also choose to carry a small copy with you as a daily reminder.

Over time, return to your Listening Oathand update it as you grow. Let it evolve with you, becoming a living reflection of your intention to listen with your heart, not just your ears.

**My Listening Oath Template**

**Today, I commit to becoming a better listener, to others, and to myself.** I recognise that true listening is an act of love, presence, and respect. Through this Oath, I pledge to:

**My Listening Promises**

- I will pause before responding, creating space for reflection.
- I will give eye contact and put away distractions.
- I will ask open-hearted questions that invite deeper connection.
- I will listen with kindness, patience, and without judgment.
- I will honour silence as part of true listening.
- I will listen to myself with the same compassion I offer others.
- I will respect the courage it takes for someone to share their truth.
- I will be curious, open, and willing to learn from others' experiences.

**My Personal Listening Intention**

*(Write one or two sentences in your own words, e.g., "I commit to listening with my heart first, and my mind second.")*

...............................................................................

...............................................................................

...........................................................

**Signature & Date**

*(sign your name as a symbol of your commitment)*

................................................... ..........................

**Signature** **Date**

## Closing Reflection

In a world that races forward and grows louder with every passing day, your choice to pause and listen is both radical and sacred. True listening is not confined to the ears; it is an offering of your whole being, your presence, your patience, your stillness, and above all, your open heart. When you listen deeply to another, you create a sanctuary where they can rest, a space where their words are not just heard but *held*. In that moment, you give them one of life's greatest gifts: the experience of being truly seen, felt, and understood, and when you turn that same listening inward, when you quiet the noise, slow your racing thoughts, and lean into your own heart, you rediscover the truth that has always lived within you. You reclaim the wisdom that busyness often buries and remember that your inner voice is worthy of trust. Listening, in its purest form, is an act of love. It dissolves walls where there was once separation. It opens doors to compassion where there was once misunderstanding. It strengthens bonds and heals wounds that words alone cannot reach. It invites empathy to flourish and reminds you that every story, every voice, every heart deserves to be received with tenderness and grace. So may your listening become your love in action. May you carry this practice into your conversations, your relationships, your work, and your own self-reflection. Let it remind you daily that silence can speak volumes, that presence is more powerful than performance, and that to listen is to give life. When you listen with your heart, you do not just hear, you connect, you heal, you transform, and in that moment, you come home to yourself and invite others to do the same.

## The Heart Leads the Way

Your heart knows the direction, even when the mind feels unsure. Another Unbound book or program will give you the tools to walk that direction with clarity and confidence – **www.timetotransform.world**

# MODULE 8 – FOCUS

**Your Opening Reflection**

**Invitation to Return to What Matters -** As you step into this module, I invite you to see focus not as rigid discipline, but as devotion. Where you place your attention is where your life gathers meaning and energy. Each moment is an invitation to return, to what matters most, to what nourishes your heart, to what brings you alive. Focus is not about perfection, it is about choosing presence over distraction, alignment over scattering, love over noise. Let this be your practice: to notice when your attention drifts, and gently bring it back, again and again, to the truth of what matters most to you.

- "Where is your attention most often directed, and does it serve your heart's true desires?"
- "What distractions most often pull you away from what matters most to your heart?"
- "When do you feel most present, and what helps you return to that state?"
- "How do your daily choices reflect (or contradict) the vision you hold for your life?"
- "If you gave your best energy to what truly nourishes you, what would shift in your life?"

Let these questions open the doorway into presence. Every answer you give, whether in words, sensations, or silence, is a bridge between where you are and where you are going.

## Learning Objectives

The learning objectives are included here to give you a clear focus for this module, ensuring that each practice you explore moves you closer to mastering the skills, insights, and heart-led awareness that will enrich your life well beyond the program. By the end of this module, you will:

- Understand how focus connects to emotional intelligence and heart-centred living
- Identify internal and external distractions and develop strategies for managing them
- Learn techniques to sharpen attention, reduce overwhelm, and stay aligned with purpose
- Practice mindfulness and time-management techniques that support deep work and mental clarity

## Core Emotional Domains

The core emotional intelligence domains covered here are essential because they form the foundation for lasting heart connection, guiding you to deepen self-awareness, regulate emotions, build resilience, and strengthen the mind-body bond throughout your *Unbound* journey.

- **Self-Awareness:** Focus begins with knowing what matters most to you. You learn to recognise when your attention drifts and what pulls you off course. Through reflection, you develop insight into your patterns of distraction and alignment, allowing you to consciously choose where to place your energy.
- **Self-Regulation:** Cultivating focus requires you to redirect your attention, moment by moment. You discover how to pause, breathe, and bring yourself back to centre. With practice, you build the inner discipline to stay grounded in your priorities without being overtaken by external noise or internal restlessness.
- **Motivation (Goal-Oriented Action):** When you focus on what matters, your purpose becomes clearer. You align your time, energy, and actions with your goals and values. Motivation grows from meaningful direction, and you begin to act not out of urgency, but from heartfelt clarity and drive.

- **Focus and Attention Control:** You develop the capacity to be fully present. Rather than scattering your energy, you train your attention like a muscle. Whether through mindful awareness or intentional routines, you learn to focus with depth, presence, and purpose.
- **Resilience and Mental Agility:** Distraction, pressure, and uncertainty are part of life. With strengthened focus, you become more mentally agile, able to adapt, re-centre, and recover from setbacks. You learn to hold your attention steady, even amidst chaos, and that is a powerful act of resilience.

### "Focus – Cultivating Presence, Purpose And Productivity"

Focus is a powerful amplifier. What you focus on expands. When you give your attention to fear, stress, or distraction, those things begin to shape your reality, but when you align your focus with love, purpose, and values, something remarkable happens, your energy becomes clearer, your actions more intentional, and your life more heart-led. In this part of your *Unbound* journey, you are invited to move away from the myth of multitasking and into the grounded clarity of presence. Focus is not about pressure or perfection. It is not about rigid control or doing more. It is about choosing, consciously, compassionately, what you give your time, energy, and emotional investment to. When your attention is centred in your heart, you naturally prioritise what truly matters. You begin to notice where your energy leaks through worry, self-doubt, or constant busyness, and instead of being scattered, you begin to return, again and again, to the present moment, where your power lives. Focus helps you see the difference between distraction and direction. It gives you the courage to say no to what drains you and yes to what nourishes you. In this space, you find the freedom to move forward with clarity, confidence, and purpose. By reclaiming your focus, you reclaim your life, not through force, but through the gentle act of presence, and from that place, your heart has the space to lead.

### Focus As A Heart-Centred Muscle: Presence Vs. Distraction

Focus is not a fixed trait you either have or lack, it is a living, breathing practice, cultivated moment by moment. Just like a muscle, it grows stronger the more you use it, but only when exercised with intention, compassion, and patience. In the modern world, where constant notifications, deadlines, and distractions demand your attention, it is easy to feel as though your focus has been stolen or scattered across a thousand different directions. This can leave you restless, anxious, and disconnected, but your heart whispers a different truth: focus is not about holding on tighter, it is about learning to return, again and again, to what matters most. When your focus is anchored in the heart, it is not driven by force or urgency, but by love and presence. Focus becomes less about finishing tasks and more about *showing up fully* for your life. This is presence, not perfection. It is not about getting everything right or keeping everything under control. Instead, it is about remembering to come back to the breath, to your body, and to the values that guide your spirit. It is about being here now, awake to what is unfolding in front of you, and willing to meet it with openness and curiosity. Distraction, in contrast, is not simply laziness or weakness, it is often a signpost pointing to unmet needs. You drift into distraction when a part of you feels unsafe, unworthy, or overwhelmed. You scroll endlessly, busy yourself with tasks, or numb your feelings because something in you is afraid of stillness. Stillness exposes truth, and that truth may feel uncomfortable. Yet the practice of focus allows you to approach this with gentleness. Every time you notice your mind wandering and guide it softly back, you are rewiring your nervous system to trust: *it is safe to be here, it is safe to be still, it is safe to be me.* This is the essence of heart-centred focus, it transforms distraction from an enemy into a teacher. Instead of battling against your wandering mind, you learn to meet it with compassion and then lovingly return. Focus is not about perfection, it is about *practice.* It is not about rigid control, it is about *flow.* It is not about denying distraction, it is about choosing devotion. When you cultivate this kind of focus, life itself changes. Your attention is no longer hijacked by every demand. You begin to listen more deeply to your inner compass. You make choices that reflect your intentions instead of your fears. You find yourself moving with the rhythm of life instead of being pulled apart by it. With practice, this focus strengthens your resilience, sharpens your clarity, and deepens your sense of connection, to yourself, to others, and to the greater pulse of existence.

Every time you return your focus to the heart, you remember who you are. You remember why you began. You remember that your attention is sacred, and where you place it shapes the quality of your entire life. Presence becomes your new rhythm, and focus becomes your quiet power, an inner strength not born from control, but from trust, and so, your practice is simple: notice when you drift. Breathe. Return. Repeat. This is how you build the muscle of focus, not through force, but through remembering,

remembering that you are safe, remembering that you are whole, and remembering that your heart already knows the way.

**Ancient Perspectives: Mindfulness (Buddhism), Eudaimonia (Aristotle), Intention (Taoism)**

The power of focus has long been revered by ancient wisdom traditions, not just as a tool for productivity, but as a sacred gateway to your purpose, balance, and inner peace. When you look at focus through the eyes of these traditions, you begin to see that it is not simply about narrowing your attention, it is about orienting your whole being toward truth, wholeness, and harmony with life itself.

<u>Mindfulness – Buddhism</u>

In Buddhism, mindfulness (*sati*) is the practice of sustained, compassionate attention. It asks you to bring your awareness fully into the present moment, whether in your breath, body, thoughts, or feelings. Here, focus is not about tightening your grip or forcing control, it is about softening into presence. You become a witness to what arises: sensations, emotions, and mental patterns. With each gentle return to the breath, you train your attention to rest in awareness itself. This act of presence is both your anchor and your liberation, it grounds you in what is real and frees you from being enslaved to every passing thought. In mindfulness, your focus becomes a bridge, between chaos and calm, fear and clarity, suffering and compassion. It is less about doing and more about being, an invitation for you to live awake.

<u>Eudaimonia – Aristotle</u>

In Aristotle's philosophy, the idea of *eudaimonia,* often translated as flourishing or living well, reminds you that the highest form of focus is not measured by efficiency or achievement, but by virtue. To live with *eudaimonia* is to align your focus with what truly matters: courage, wisdom, integrity, and kindness. Here, your focus is not scattered among endless desires but directed toward what makes life meaningful. It is an ethical alignment, where your energy and attention are devoted to cultivating excellence of character. When you live with this kind of focused intentionality, your daily actions become infused with purpose. You stop chasing fleeting rewards and begin embodying values that endure. Focus, in Aristotle's teaching, is not simply mental, it is moral. It is your devotion to living in such a way that your life becomes a reflection of your inner truth.

Intention – Taoism

In Taoism, you are invited to understand focus through the lens of *yi*, intention, or the clarity of your heart's aim. Unlike Western ideas of discipline that emphasise force or willpower, Taoist wisdom encourages you to align your focus with the effortless flow of the Tao, "the Way." Here, focus is not about pushing harder, but about listening deeper. You learn to attune to the natural rhythm of life, to sense when to act and when to be still. Intention in Taoism is never divorced from harmony, it arises from simplicity, sincerity, and balance. When your heart is clear, your actions become spontaneous and fluid, as natural as water finding its path. Your focus then becomes graceful, responsive, and alive, not rigid. In this way, focus is not a burden you must maintain but a gift of alignment with the greater whole.

The Integration

These ancient traditions together remind you that true focus is not a clenched state of mental effort, it is a sacred state of alignment. When your attention rests in mindfulness, when your choices reflect your deepest virtues, and when your intentions flow from presence and peace, your focus is transformed. It becomes more than attention, it becomes reverence. A way of walking through the world awake. A practice of living with awareness, purpose, and love.

## The Neuroscience Of Attention And How Focus Strengthens Resilience

Focus is not just a mental habit, it is a living biological process grounded in the very architecture of your brain. When you begin to understand the neuroscience of attention, you realise that presence, clarity, and resilience are not fixed traits but trainable capacities. Just like a muscle, your focus grows stronger the more you nurture it with awareness, practice, and compassion. At the centre of this process is your **prefrontal cortex**, the *"executive hub"* of your brain. This region governs planning, decision-making, emotional regulation, and the ability to stay aligned with your long-term goals. Every time you direct your attention toward a single task, value, or intention, your prefrontal cortex activates more strongly. It filters distractions, prioritises what matters, and stabilises your emotional state. In moments of chaos or uncertainty, this kind of focus acts like an anchor, giving you clarity when everything around you feels turbulent, but focus is not simply concentration, it is also the foundation of emotional resilience. When you train your attention through mindfulness, breathwork, or intentional rituals, you begin to shift activity away from the **amygdala**, the part of your brain wired for fear and reactivity. Instead, you strengthen neural pathways associated with calm, regulation, and perspective. Science confirms that sustained attention lowers stress hormones such as cortisol, reduces over-reactivity, and increases **neuroplasticity**, your brain's remarkable ability to rewire itself. With each practice of returning to your breath or your heart, you are literally sculpting a more resilient nervous system.

Focus also awakens your brain's natural reward system. Every time you devote yourself to something meaningful, your brain releases **dopamine**, a neurotransmitter linked with motivation, hope, and a sense of accomplishment. This creates a feedback loop: the more you focus, the more energised and empowered you feel, which in turn reinforces your ability to continue. This is why people who cultivate focus often recover more quickly from setbacks, they know how to guide their attention back to what matters instead of spiralling into overwhelm. In a world flooded with noise and distraction, choosing to focus becomes an act of **inner leadership**. Each time you say, "*This is what I will give my energy to*," you are reprogramming your nervous system. You are teaching your brain and body that peace is possible, that clarity is within reach, and that you are capable of guiding yourself through life with strength and balance. At its essence, focus is not about force, it is about **return**. Returning to your breath when your mind wanders. Returning to your values when you feel pulled in every direction. Returning to your heart when fear or doubt threatens to take over. With each return, you are not failing, you are building resilience. You are carving new pathways in your brain that remind you, even in difficulty, that your heart knows the way home.

### The Link Between Focused Intention And Emotional Regulation

Focused intention is far more than setting goals, it is a practice of choosing, moment by moment, where your energy and awareness will rest. It is the art of alignment: bringing your attention into harmony with your deepest values and your heart's truth. When your focus is anchored in clarity, honesty, and presence, you do more than sharpen your thinking, you begin to regulate your emotions with grace and strength. When you feel emotionally dysregulated, anxious, reactive, overwhelmed, it is often because your attention has been scattered or hijacked. Your mind leaps from fear to distraction, dragging your nervous system along with it. Yet the moment you consciously redirect your focus back to an anchor, your breath, a grounding phrase, a meaningful purpose, you reclaim your inner authority. This deliberate return activates your prefrontal cortex, the part of your brain responsible for calm, decision-making, and perspective, and creates space between stimulus and response. That space is where emotional regulation lives. Setting a focused intention such as *"I choose peace"* or *"I remain steady and present"* is not just symbolic, it is neurological. Research in neuroscience shows that when you guide your attention deliberately, you decrease amygdala activity (the brain's fear and reactivity centre) while strengthening neural connections in areas tied to self-awareness, regulation, and compassion. In essence, you are teaching your brain to return to balance. Emotionally intelligent people are not those who feel less, they often feel more deeply, but they cultivate the ability to pause, to notice, and to guide their emotions instead of being swept away by them.

In your *Unbound* journey, focused intention becomes a compass. It anchors you in the centre of chaos and reminds you that your emotions are not enemies to be suppressed, but messengers to be listened to. By meeting them with awareness and compassion, and then returning again and again to your chosen focus, you build a stable foundation within yourself. Over time, this practice transforms reactivity into responsiveness, confusion into clarity, and vulnerability into resilience. With each intentional return, you strengthen your emotional muscles. Your reactions soften. Your clarity deepens, and your resilience expands. Focused intention becomes more than a mental skill, it is a spiritual discipline that allows you to meet life not from fear or habit, but from the steady, unwavering truth of your heart.

### Aligning Daily Actions With Core Values And Long-Term Purpose

Focus becomes powerful when it is not just about productivity, but about alignment. In your *Unbound* journey, alignment means this: your daily choices reflect your deepest values and your highest intentions. You move through life not reacting to the noise of the world, but guided by the quiet truth of your heart. To live in alignment is to wake each day with clarity about what matters most to you, and then honour that truth through your actions. This is not always easy in a world filled with distractions, deadlines, and competing demands, but when your actions mirror your values, you experience a sense of integrity, wholeness, and inner peace. Your **core values,** love, kindness, freedom, honesty, compassion, creativity, are the compass points of your soul. Your **long-term purpose** is your north star. When you lose focus or feel emotionally unbalanced, it is often because your daily life has drifted from these inner truths. The remedy is not to do more, but to realign. Ask yourself each morning:

- What do I want to stand for today?
- How can I bring my values into this next moment, this next task?
- Will my actions today serve the life I truly want to build?

When you pause to reflect on these questions, you begin to notice where your energy is being drained by obligations that do not serve you, or habits that dull your spirit. You can then begin to shift, gently but decisively, towards choices that nourish your purpose and reflect your integrity. This is the practice of **conscious focus**: not striving harder, but living more truly. Over time, these small acts of alignment build momentum. You find yourself saying yes to what is essential, and no to what is merely urgent. You begin to trust your inner guidance, and your life becomes a reflection of your deepest truth. In this module, you are invited to reclaim your focus not just as mental concentration, but as soulful intention. When your daily actions align with your core values and your long-term purpose, you do not just stay on track, you come home to yourself.

**Daily Focus Ritual**

Focus does not just happen, it is something you cultivate with intention. By creating a simple, personal ritual, you can train your mind and heart to return to what truly matters, even in a world filled with noise and distraction. This ritual is not about perfection, but about presence. It is about honouring your time, your energy, and your values by choosing where your attention goes. Your daily focus ritual might include:

- **Setting a clear intention each morning:** Begin your day by asking, *What truly matters today?* Write it down, breathe it in, and carry it with you.
- **Blocking out specific times for focused tasks:** Protect small windows of uninterrupted time, even 25–50 minutes, where your energy is devoted to one meaningful activity.
- **Creating phone-free zones or hours:** Free yourself from constant notifications. Whether it is during meals, first thing in the morning, or before bed, gift yourself undistracted presence.

- **Dedicating time to deep, undistracted work:** Choose one priority project and give it your full attention. Let this be your daily act of devotion to what matters most.
- **Ending your day with a short reflection or review:** Ask yourself, *Where did my focus serve me well today? Where did it wander? What will I choose tomorrow?*

Now, write out your personal focus ritual in a way that feels realistic, supportive, and empowering. Keep it simple enough to follow daily, yet meaningful enough to inspire you.

Commit to practicing your ritual for the next 3 days. Notice what shifts, both inside and out, when you treat your focus as something sacred. You may find that you move through your day with more clarity, more energy, and a deeper sense of alignment with your heart.

**Case Study Discussion: Archie's Journey**

Archie was a very bright and ambitious student, but he found himself struggling to complete his university degree. He had always been passionate about his field of study, but his inability to focus was hindering his progress. Archie was really determined to overcome this, and he embarked on a journey of self–discovery and personal growth. We began by analysing his daily routines and identifying distractions, of which there were many. Social media, constant notifications, and his own wandering thoughts were stealing his attention. After discussing a few options, Archie chose to implement a few strict time management strategies. He created a dedicated study schedule, allocating specific hours for focused work, and minimising interruptions. To further enhance his concentration, Archie explored meditation and mindfulness techniques. He practiced meditation, learning to quiet his mind and bring his attention back to the present moment. This newfound ability to anchor himself in the task at hand proved invaluable. In time, Archie noticed a significant improvement. His coursework became more manageable, and his marks started to rise. The more he practiced focusing, the easier it became. He tapped into his passion for learning, finding joy in deep engagement with his studies. Archie's newfound focus not only helped him complete his degree but also transformed his overall approach to life. He became more disciplined, productive, and confident in his abilities. As he embarked on his career, the skills he acquired in focusing served as a foundation for success in all aspects of his life. In the end, Archie's journey taught him that focus was not just a means to an end, but a life skill that unlocked his true potential and allowed him to live his best life.

**Reflective Exercise: Archie's Journey**

Here are four profound and reflective questions inspired by Archie's story to help you engage with your own focus journey:

1. *Like Archie, what daily distractions, whether digital, mental, or emotional, are pulling you away from what truly matters?* Archie realised that notifications, social media, and scattered thoughts were silently draining his energy. What do you need to acknowledge or change to reclaim your focus?
2. *Archie reconnected with his passion through deep engagement, when have you last felt fully immersed in something meaningful?* Think back to a time when you were completely present and alive in your work or study. What helped you get there, and how could you invite that feeling back?
3. *What would it look like for you to create structure and boundaries around your time, like Archie did, to support your growth and purpose?* Archie found freedom in discipline. Could a simple schedule or focus ritual help you honour your goals more consistently?
4. *Archie used mindfulness to quiet his mind and return to the present moment, how could you bring more presence into your day?* Whether through meditation, deep breathing, or mindful pauses, how might you anchor yourself in the now and bring calm clarity to whatever you are doing?

### Affirmations For You – (Heart Whispers)

Affirmations have the power to quiet the noise of doubt, open the doorway to self-trust, and draw you back into the wisdom of your heart. When practised daily, they nurture an inner dialogue based in love and truth, helping you live each day more aligned with who you truly are. I invite you to repeat silently or write:

- *I prioritise my tasks to maintain focus and productivity.*
- *I eliminate distractions to sharpen my focus on the present.*
- *I practice mindfulness to cultivate a centred and focused mind.*
- *I set clear goals to keep my focus aligned and purposeful.*

- *I train my mind to block out noise and maintain focus.*
- *I return my attention gently each time my mind wanders, building strength with every breath.*
- *I focus on what truly matters and release what does not serve my highest good.*

**"The 5-Minute Focused Breath"**

I invite you to find a comfortable position, allowing your body to settle and your breath to become steady. Gently close your eyes and turn your awareness inward. As you begin the guided Focus meditation, allow yourself to notice the rhythm of your breathing, each inhale drawing you into presence, each exhale releasing tension and distraction. For the next five minutes, your breath will be your anchor. Thoughts may come, emotions may rise, or your attention may drift, that is natural. The practice is not about staying perfectly focused, but about noticing when your mind has wandered and gently returning to your breath. Each return is an act of strengthening, a moment of resilience, a reminder that focus is less about force and more about remembering. At the conclusion of the meditation, I invite you to reflect with honesty and curiosity:

- *How many times did your mind drift?*
- *What helped you return?*
- *Did you notice a shift in your body, your emotions, or your clarity of mind as you practiced returning?*

Carry this awareness into the rest of your day. Remember, every time you guide yourself back, you are training your mind and heart to focus with greater ease. With each return, you are building not just concentration, but presence, patience, and peace.

## Closing Reflection

Focus is more than concentration, it is a return to what matters most. Archie's journey reminds you that the ability to direct your attention is not something you are born with fully formed, but a living skill. It can be learned, practiced, refined, and strengthened with intention. Every time you bring yourself back from distraction, you are building a muscle of presence and resilience. When you choose focus, you are choosing to honour your time, your energy, and your dreams. You begin to sift through the noise of demands and distractions, clearing a path to what is meaningful. In that clarity, you discover that focus is not about doing more, it is about doing what matters with depth, devotion, and heart. This practice reminds you that your attention is sacred. Where your attention goes, your energy flows. Each moment you bring your full presence to something, whether it is a task, a conversation, or a quiet breath, you are reclaiming your life from fragmentation and returning it to wholeness. Focus is not about perfection. It is about return. Return to your breath, to your values, to your purpose. Return to what lights you up and grounds you in truth. Each return is a victory, a small act of courage, and a reminder that you are free to choose again. As you close this reflection, may you carry forward the knowing that focus is not pressure, but permission. Permission to live in alignment. Permission to give your best attention to what you love. Permission to let go of the noise and turn toward the voice of your heart. Focus is the path home,back to clarity, back to presence, back to what truly matters.

**Continue the Courage**

The courage you showed in reading this module deserves to grow. The Unbound journey offers more guidance, more breakthroughs, and more moments that remind you what you are capable of – www.timetotransform.world

Time To Transform

EMPOWERING LIVES

Return to Purpose

Part 3

# PART 3 – RETURN TO PURPOSE AND THE HUMAN MEANING OF LAW

**(Time to Transform: Living Unbound - Chapters 10 Forgiveness • 28 Reflection • 29 Homecoming • 12 Kindness)**

Law is a profession of consequence. Every decision carries weight. Every matter leaves a trace, on clients, institutions, communities, and on the lawyer who carries it. Over time, the accumulation is unavoidable. Even the most principled practice exposes lawyers to loss, disappointment, injustice, and moral tension. This section exists because without conscious integration, that accumulation hardens. The four modules in this final movement, **Forgiveness, Reflection, Homecoming, and Kindness**, were chosen to address what the law does to the practitioner over time, not through failure, but through sustained responsibility. They are not corrective measures; they are practices of restoration. They ensure that the lawyer can remain ethically grounded, emotionally clear, and connected to purpose across a lifetime of practice. This is where the long view is taken.

### Why These Modules Matter in Legal Life

**Forgiveness** is included because unresolved residue undermines judgment. Lawyers are exposed to conflict, regret, and outcomes that do not sit easily with conscience. Without forgiveness, of others, of systems, and of oneself, resentment accumulates. This module provides a disciplined process for releasing what no longer serves clarity, allowing lawyers to continue practising without carrying bitterness or self-reproach into future matters. Forgiveness here is not absolution. It is professional hygiene.

**Reflection** restores ethical calibration. The pace of legal work rarely allows space to pause, examine, or integrate experience. Yet reflection is where learning becomes wisdom. This module strengthens the capacity to review decisions, conduct, and outcomes without self-justification or self-attack. It enables lawyers to remain accountable to their values while continuing to evolve their practice. Reflection is not retreat from responsibility. It is its refinement.

**Homecoming** addresses disconnection. Over time, many lawyers drift from the values that originally drew them to the profession. Homecoming is the deliberate return to those values, justice, service, fairness, dignity, not as ideals, but as lived commitments. This module reconnects the lawyer to a sense of internal alignment, ensuring that practice reflects conviction rather than habit. This is where the law becomes personal again, without becoming personal inappropriately.

**Kindness** is the final discipline, and the most demanding. Kindness in law is not indulgence. It is restraint, respect, and humanity exercised in contexts that often reward hardness. This module reframes kindness as a professional strength, the capacity to wield authority without cruelty, to advocate firmly without dehumanising, and to lead without diminishing others. Kindness protects the integrity of justice, and the lawyer who serves it.

### When to Return to This Section

This section is particularly relevant when:

- disappointment, cynicism, or moral injury begins to surface
- the original sense of purpose feels distant or obscured
- regret, anger, or accumulated emotional residue interferes with clarity
- success feels increasingly hollow or misaligned
- you want to practise ethically, not merely strategically

These moments are not failures. They are signals that integration is required.

### The Deeper Purpose of Section Three

Legal success is often measured externally, outcomes achieved, reputations built, positions held, but legacy is shaped internally. Section Three exists to ensure that success does not come at the cost of integrity, and that endurance does not replace meaning. It reconnects the lawyer with justice as a human value, not merely a technical outcome, and with law as a vocation that carries moral weight as well as professional obligation. Here, you are reminded that how you practise matters as much as what you achieve. This section does not ask you to abandon ambition or rigour. It asks you to practise with conscience intact, to ensure that over time, the law refines rather than diminishes the person entrusted to uphold it. This is where a career in law becomes a life in law.

# MODULE 9 – FORGIVENESS

## Your Opening Reflection

**An Invitation to Forgive -** As you enter this module, give yourself permission to soften and open. Forgiveness is not about excusing the past, but about freeing your heart in the present. With each breath, allow yourself to release a little of the weight you have been carrying. Let this be a moment to imagine what it feels like to live lighter, to choose compassion over resentment, and to offer yourself the healing gift of peace.

- "What is one hurt you have been holding onto, and what would it feel like to release it?"
- "How has holding onto resentment or pain affected your life, relationships, or health?"
- "If you forgave fully, how might your heart and spirit feel lighter?"
- "What beliefs do you have about forgiveness that might be keeping you from it?"
- "How might forgiveness be a gift you give yourself, not just to the other person?"
- "What is one small step you can take today toward forgiving someone or yourself?"
- "Is there someone you still need to forgive, including yourself?"

Let these questions open the doorway into presence. Every answer you give, whether in words, sensations, or silence, is a bridge between where you are and where you are going.

## Learning Objectives

The learning objectives are included here to give you a clear focus for this module, ensuring that each practice you explore moves you closer to mastering the skills, insights, and heart-led awareness that will enrich your life well beyond the program. By the end of this module, you will:

- Define forgiveness and differentiate it from enabling or excusing behavior.
- Understand how forgiveness promotes emotional healing and inner peace.
- Reflect on personal barriers to self-forgiveness and forgiveness of others.
- Apply practical techniques to begin the process of releasing resentment.
- Recognise forgiveness as a path to deeper heart connection and emotional resilience.

## Core Emotional Domains

The core emotional intelligence domains covered here are essential because they form the foundation for lasting heart connection, guiding you to deepen self-awareness, regulate emotions, build resilience, and strengthen the mind-body bond throughout your *Unbound* journey.

- **Self-Awareness:** You learn to recognise the emotions, memories, and narratives that keep resentment or pain alive.
- **Self-Regulation:** Forgiveness invites you to respond to hurt with intention rather than reactivity, creating space for peace.
- **Empathy:** You begin to understand the pain of others without excusing harm, building compassion while maintaining boundaries.
- **Social Skills:** Releasing blame creating healthier relationships, clearer communication, and deeper trust.
- **Motivation:** Forgiveness becomes a path to emotional freedom, inspiring you to grow beyond the wound and reclaim your energy.

## "Forgiveness – Releasing The Past"

Forgiveness as Inner Liberation. Forgiveness is not a gift you give to someone who wronged you, it is a sacred act of release that you offer to yourself. It is not about excusing harm, forgetting pain, or pretending it did not happen. True forgiveness is an inner act of liberation, a conscious choice to unhook your heart from the weight of resentment, anger, and emotional toxicity. When you hold onto hurt, your body holds it too. Your breath tightens, your thoughts loop, your nervous system stays alert to an old danger. Over time, this pain calcifies, not just in your memory, but in your spirit. Forgiveness does not erase the wound, but it tends to it with compassion, allowing you to heal from the inside out. To forgive is to reclaim your peace. It is a declaration that your wellbeing matters more than your grudges. It is the courage to soften a hardened heart, not for their sake, but for your freedom. In forgiveness, you open a door to emotional clarity, spaciousness, and even gratitude for how far you have come. You stop letting the past define your present. You choose to grow. You choose to feel light again, and most powerfully, you realise: *Forgiveness is not something they have to earn, it is something you decide to live.*

## The Psychology and Spirituality Of Forgiveness

Forgiveness sits at the crossroads of psychology and spirituality, bridging the science of healing with the soul's deep longing for peace. From a psychological perspective, forgiveness is a transformative emotional process, one that invites you to meet your pain with courage rather than avoidance. It begins by acknowledging the reality of what happened: the wound, the injustice, the betrayal. This is not about denial, suppression, or pretending it did not matter. It is about facing the truth with both clarity and self-compassion. In this space, you are not asked to condone, excuse, or forget harmful behavior. Instead, forgiveness becomes an intentional act of reclaiming your mental and emotional freedom. It is a conscious decision to stop letting the hurt dictate your inner world. Research consistently shows that practicing forgiveness can significantly lower cortisol levels, ease symptoms of depression and anxiety, improve cardiovascular health, and strengthen immune function. Psychologically, it disrupts cycles of rumination, anger, and resentment that keep you tethered to the past. Forgiveness replaces reactive survival responses with grounded emotional regulation, helping you think, feel, and respond from a place of clarity rather than pain. In choosing to forgive, you are not giving power back to the person who hurt you, you are reclaiming it for yourself. You shift from being defined by what happened to being empowered by how you respond. Far from being a sign of weakness, forgiveness reflects deep emotional intelligence: the capacity to sit with pain, understand your emotions, integrate the lessons, and still act from your highest self. Forgiveness is not the closing of a chapter; it is the opening of a lighter, freer one, one in which your past no longer dictates the limits of your joy.

The Spirituality of Forgiveness

Spiritually, forgiveness is a sacred and transformative act, a gentle unraveling of bitterness, fear, and the invisible threads that bind you to past pain. It is not a forgetting, but a remembering: that within your heart resides the vast capacity to hold both grief and grace, to honour the truth of your wounds while still choosing love. Across spiritual traditions, forgiveness is often more than a single act; it is a lifelong path, a pilgrimage back to wholeness. In Christianity, forgiveness reflects the essence of divine mercy, an invitation to mirror the compassion and unconditional love of God, even when it feels undeserved. In Buddhism, it is a practice of letting go of attachments to anger and resentment, releasing the suffering that binds both self and others. In Indigenous wisdom, forgiveness is woven into the fabric of community, restoring harmony and balance not only between people, but between the land, the ancestors, and the spirit world. In each of these traditions, forgiveness is not a transaction or an act of surrendering power, it is an act of transcendence. It lifts you above the smallness of the wound and returns you to the vastness of your true self. It is a declaration that your identity is not defined by the harm you have suffered, but by the love you choose to embody. To forgive is to say with conviction: *This story will not define me. My heart is larger than this wound.* It is a spiritual commitment to inner peace, a conscious decision to stop rehearsing and re-enacting the hurt, and a willingness to live open-hearted in a world that sometimes shatters hearts. In the end, forgiveness is not only about setting someone else free, it is about liberating your own soul so it can move without the weight of the past, ready to love again without fear.

### The Effects Of Resentment On Physical And Emotional Health

Resentment may seem like an invisible weight, hidden beneath the surface, tucked behind a polite smile, or pushed down in the name of strength, but over time, it becomes one of the most corrosive emotions you carry, impacting both your physical health and emotional wellbeing in deep and far-reaching ways.

Emotional Toll: Living in a Loop of Pain

Resentment is not just a passing emotion, it is a sustained state of unresolved hurt entwined with a sense of injustice. It keeps you locked in mental replays, revisiting conversations, events, and missed opportunities for closure. The mind becomes a theatre of "*what ifs*" and "*should haves*," looping the same scene over and over. This constant rumination activates the stress response repeatedly, leaving your nervous system in a perpetual state of low-grade tension. You might notice yourself feeling on edge for no clear reason, or withdrawing emotionally because the hurt feels too raw to face. Over time, resentment shrinks your emotional world; joy feels distant, trust feels risky, and even moments of peace are interrupted by a lingering ache. Without release, it quietly shapes how you see yourself, others, and life itself.

Physical Toll: The Body Remembers

The mind may replay the wound, but the body stores it. Science confirms that chronic emotional stress, like the kind resentment breeds, takes a measurable toll on physical health. Elevated cortisol can disrupt the delicate balance of your immune, digestive, and cardiovascular systems. Sleep becomes shallow, muscles tighten like armour, and your breath unconsciously shortens, signalling to your body that danger is still present. Over months or years, this state of guardedness increases inflammation, slows healing, and leaves you more vulnerable to illness. Resentment does not just live in your thoughts; it settles in your shoulders, your jaw, your gut. It can become an unseen weight you carry everywhere, one that erodes vitality and keeps the body in a constant state of readiness for a battle that never arrives.

What Makes Resentment So Draining?

Resentment drains you because it demands constant energy to sustain. It is like keeping a fire smouldering, you must continually add emotional fuel in the form of rumination, anger, or silent bitterness. This emotional maintenance prevents you from fully engaging with the present, because part of you is still anchored in the past, guarding the wound. The cost is high: hope dims, creativity dries up, and compassion, for yourself and others, becomes harder to access. Resentment consumes the very qualities that make life rich and meaningful. It convinces you that holding on protects you, when in truth, it only keeps you tethered to pain.

The Healing Choice: Letting Go Does Not Excuse, It Releases

Letting go of resentment is an act of courage, not concession. It is not about pretending the harm never happened or absolving someone of responsibility, it is about reclaiming your freedom from the grip of the past. Letting go means loosening your identity from the story of hurt, so you are no longer defined by it. It is choosing to end the cycle of self-punishment and allowing your energy to flow toward what restores and nourishes you. When you release resentment, you create space for peace to take root, for joy to return, and for your heart to open again, stronger, wiser, and unburdened. As you begin to release resentment, through self-reflection, compassion, and forgiveness, you reclaim your emotional vitality and physical wellbeing. You begin to return to yourself, because resentment does not protect your heart. It holds it hostage and healing begins when you set it free.

### Forgiveness vs. Excusing Behavior

One of the greatest misunderstandings about forgiveness is the belief that to forgive someone is to excuse or justify what they did, but true forgiveness is not about erasing the past, it is about releasing *yourself* from being held hostage by it.

<u>Excusing Behaviour Means Minimising Harm</u>

When you excuse someone's behaviour, you downplay the impact of their actions. You might say "*It was not that bad,*" or "*They did not mean it.*" Excusing can lead to bypassing accountability, suppressing your truth, or staying silent in the name of keeping the peace. It can invalidate your feelings, create confusion about your worth, and even enable unhealthy dynamics to continue. Excusing often arises from a desire to avoid conflict, or from internalised beliefs that your pain is not valid,but your hurt matters. Your boundaries matter. Healing begins when you name what was true.

<u>Forgiveness, on the Other Hand, Is a Conscious Release</u>

Forgiveness does not erase the wrong, it **honours that it happened** and still chooses to let go of the emotional grip it has over you. It does **not** mean you condone the behaviour or pretend it did not cause harm. It means you are no longer willing to carry the bitterness, anger, or resentment that weighs on your heart. Forgiveness says:

- *"I am choosing peace over pain."*
- *"I no longer want to re-live what hurt me."*
- *"I will not allow this to define my future."*

It may involve setting boundaries. It may mean walking away. It may mean holding someone accountable, with love and clarity, but without vengeance.

Forgiveness Empowers, Excusing Disempowers

Forgiveness is an act of reclamation, it hands you back the keys to your own heart. When you forgive, you release the hold the past has over your present, and in doing so, you restore your agency. Your emotional energy is no longer drained by replaying the wound; instead, it becomes available for creating the life you want. Forgiveness clears the fog of resentment, allowing you to see yourself and your future with greater clarity. It is the choice to stand in your own sovereignty, no longer defined by someone else's actions. Excusing, however, is different. When you excuse harmful behaviour without addressing its impact, you bypass your own truth. You may shrink yourself to avoid conflict, rationalise what is unacceptable, or bury your pain in the hope that it will disappear. This often leads to cycles of guilt, self-doubt, and disempowerment, because you have abandoned your own boundaries. Forgiveness does not say, *"What happened was fine."* It says, *"What happened hurt, but I am choosing to heal. I am no longer tethered to that hurt."* It is the conscious decision to honour your worth, hold your boundaries, and live free from the emotional weight of the past. That shift, from *"It is okay"* to *"I am okay now"*, is everything. It is the difference between silencing yourself and liberating yourself.

**Effects Of Resentment On Physical And Emotional Health**

Resentment is one of the most corrosive emotions we carry, quietly building in the background, often masked as strength or righteousness, while slowly depleting your emotional reserves and affecting your physical wellbeing.

Emotionally: Resentment Traps You in the Past

Resentment is unresolved hurt wrapped in anger and replayed over time. When you hold onto it, your mind stays tethered to the original wound, replaying the story again and again. You might relive the betrayal, reimagine the argument, or rehearse what you wish you had said. This mental looping fuels anxiety, irritability, sadness, and emotional exhaustion. Resentment also blocks empathy and connection. It can harden your heart, make trust difficult, and cause emotional distancing in relationships. Over time, it narrows your worldview and disconnects you from joy, creativity, and peace. It is not just the event that causes harm, it is the ongoing emotional investment in *what was*, rather than what could be.

Physically: The Body Keeps the Score

The stress of resentment does not just live in your thoughts, it settles in your body. Chronic resentment can:

- Raise cortisol (the body's primary stress hormone)
- Disrupt sleep patterns
- Weaken your immune system
- Increase inflammation, linked to diseases such as heart disease and arthritis
- Contribute to headaches, digestive issues, and chronic fatigue

Because your nervous system cannot tell the difference between a past event and a current threat, it reacts as if you are still under attack every time you ruminate.

- Your muscles tense.
- Your breath shortens.
- Your heart rate elevates.

The result? You live in a state of low-grade, persistent fight-or-flight, even when the original danger is long gone.

The Hidden Cost: It Steals Your Present

The price of holding onto resentment extends far beyond your physical health, it quietly robs you of the life you are living right now. Every moment spent replaying the past is a moment stolen from the present. Resentment narrows your emotional landscape, reducing your capacity for joy, compassion, creativity, and peace. It colours the way you see others, the way you interpret their actions, and even the way you speak to yourself. Over time, resentment can become strangely familiar, almost comfortable in its predictability. You may find yourself returning to it like a well-worn story, not because it serves you, but because it is known. Yet, in clinging to it, you limit your own growth and dim the light of your spirit. Resentment may feel like self-protection, but it is often self-imprisonment.

The Antidote: Forgiveness and Emotional Release

Letting go of resentment does not mean erasing what happened or excusing the harm. It means choosing freedom over fixation. Forgiveness in this sense is not an act of surrender to the person who hurt you, it is a profound act of allegiance to yourself. It is a conscious choice to stop allowing the wound to dictate your emotional climate. This release is a process, often unfolding in layers. Self-awareness helps you recognise where the pain still lives in you. Breathwork can help regulate your nervous system, allowing your body to begin loosening its grip on stored tension. Compassion, both for yourself and others, softens the sharp edges of hurt, and forgiveness, when it comes, is the opening of the heart's gate, letting peace and possibility flow back in. Here, forgiveness is not about making someone else feel better. It is about reclaiming your wellbeing, clarity, and wholeness. When you release resentment, you create space, space for health, for love, for deeper connection, and for the future you truly deserve. It is not about forgetting your story; it is about writing the next chapter with a freer, lighter hand.

**How Self-Forgiveness Cultivates Compassion And Authenticity**

<u>Self-Forgiveness: The Courage to Be Whole</u>

Self-forgiveness is one of the most profound and courageous acts of emotional intelligence because it requires you to face yourself fully, your actions, your intentions, your mistakes, without turning away. It is not about denying responsibility or avoiding accountability. Instead, it is about loosening the grip of the harsh, unrelenting judgment you hold against yourself. It is allowing your humanity to breathe again. When you forgive yourself, you are not only releasing the weight of what you did; you are dismantling the limiting story you have been carrying about who you are because of it. You create the space for a truer narrative to emerge, one grounded in growth, learning, and the ongoing possibility of change. This is how self-forgiveness becomes an act of liberation, setting you free from the chains of your own self-condemnation.

<u>Self-Forgiveness Awakens Compassion</u>

You cannot offer authentic compassion to others if you cannot extend it inward. Self-forgiveness is the softening of your inner landscape, it turns the voice of your inner critic into one of understanding, wisdom, and care. It is the gentle reminder that you are not defined solely by your worst moments, but also by your capacity to rise from them. Through self-forgiveness, you stop seeing yourself as broken, unworthy, or irredeemable. Instead, you begin to recognise that mistakes, regrets, and imperfections are not flaws that exile you from love, they are the very evidence of being human. You learn to hold yourself with the same patience, empathy, and grace you would offer to a dear friend who has stumbled but longs to walk again. As your self-compassion deepens, so too does your compassion for others. You become less reactive, less judgmental, and more present. You begin to see the shared vulnerability that binds us all, the truth that we are all imperfect, all learning, and all worthy of forgiveness, and in this shared humanity, connection becomes easier, relationships grow richer, and peace takes root within you.

**Forgiveness Across Cultures And Faiths: From The Teachings Of Jesus To Buddhist Metta**

Forgiveness is not just a personal or psychological act, it is a spiritual practice embedded in the wisdom of cultures and religions across the world. While the language may differ, the invitation is the same: release what binds you, and return to love. Across traditions, forgiveness is viewed not as weakness, but as a courageous path to peace, reconciliation, and transformation, both within oneself and in relationship with others.

<u>Christianity: Forgiveness as Divine Mercy and Human Responsibility</u>

In Christianity, forgiveness is not a suggestion, it is a sacred calling. Grounded in the life and teachings of Jesus, forgiveness lies at the very heart of spiritual practice. It is seen as both a divine gift freely given and a human responsibility freely chosen. Jesus taught his followers to pray, *"Forgive us our trespasses, as we forgive those who trespass against us."* (Matthew 6:12) In this prayer, forgiveness is presented as a reciprocal act: *as we are forgiven, we must forgive.* It is not conditional on someone deserving it, it is anchored in the deeper reality that we are all in need of grace. Jesus himself modelled radical forgiveness, even in the face of betrayal, injustice, and violence. As he hung on the cross, he prayed, *"Father, forgive them, for they do not know what they are doing."* (Luke 23:34) This moment is not just one of divine mercy, it is a powerful call for all people to extend compassion even when deeply wronged. In this tradition, forgiveness is an act of moral courage, not moral weakness. It means letting go of vengeance and the right to retaliate, and choosing instead the path of mercy, reconciliation, and peace. It is a way to break cycles of harm and open the door to transformation, not just for the offender, but for the one forgiving. Forgiveness in Christianity also reflects God's nature. It is how human beings are invited to mirror divine love:

- Love that restores rather than punishes.
- Love that redeems rather than rejects.

- Love that says, *"You are not the sum of your mistakes, you are the beloved."*

At its core, Christian forgiveness affirms that every soul is capable of redemption, and that healing, personal and communal, is made possible when you choose mercy over judgment, and grace over resentment. In this light, forgiveness is not simply a response to wrongdoing. It is a spiritual pathway to freedom, and the highest expression of love.

Buddhism: Forgiveness Through Metta and Non-Attachment

In the Buddhist tradition, forgiveness is not framed as a moral duty, but as a path to liberation from suffering. It is deeply grounded in the practice of *metta,* a Pali word often translated as loving-kindness or boundless friendliness. Metta is the intentional cultivation of unconditional goodwill toward all beings, yourself, your loved ones, strangers, and even those who have caused you harm. It arises not from obligation, but from the understanding that every sentient being seeks happiness and freedom from suffering. This includes those who act unskillfully due to their own ignorance, pain, or confusion. In Buddhism, forgiveness is not about forgetting, excusing, or denying harm. It is about releasing the grip of anger, hatred, or resentment from your own heart. Holding onto these emotions is understood to create more suffering, not just for others, but for you. The Buddha taught that clinging to anger is like "*grasping a hot coal with the intent of throwing it at someone else, you are the one who gets burned.*" Through mindfulness (*sati*) and compassion (*karuṇā*), practitioners are guided to see painful emotions clearly, without judgment. You learn to observe the story of hurt with spaciousness, not resistance. Over time, this awareness softens your inner experience, and with it, your reactivity. This is where non-attachment comes in, not as indifference, but as the ability to witness your pain without becoming it. By letting go of your identification with the wound, you begin to touch a deeper truth: you are not your suffering. You are the awareness beneath it. Forgiveness, then, becomes a skillful means (upaya), a wise response that helps you let go of the inner burdens that keep you bound. It is not about changing the past. It is about freeing yourself from its emotional hold so you can return to equanimity, clarity, and compassion. In this tradition, forgiveness is not a one-time act but a practice, a gentle turning toward your own pain with the intention of healing. Buddhist monks and lay practitioners often use *metta* phrases such as:

- May I be safe.

- May I be happy.
- May I be free from suffering.
- May you be free from the suffering that causes harm.

By repeating these phrases, even toward those who have harmed you, you train your heart to let go, not to approve of harm, but to reclaim your peace and wisdom. Ultimately, in Buddhism, forgiveness is not an external transaction. It is an inner purification, a conscious path to liberation through compassion, non-attachment, and deep inner peace.

**Forgiveness Letter Exercise**

I invite you to create space, take a few deep breaths, and write two letters that hold the power to lighten your heart:

1. **To Yourself:** Write as though you are speaking to a dear friend who has walked through the same mistakes, regrets, or self-judgments you carry.
    - Express compassion: acknowledge the pain you have felt without judgment.
    - Offer understanding: recognise the circumstances, emotions, and humanity behind your actions or choices.
    - Extend release: let go of the weight of harsh self-criticism and affirm that you are worthy of love, acceptance, and peace.
2. **To Someone You Need to Forgive:** This letter is for your own healing, whether or not you ever share it.
    - Acknowledge what happened and how it impacted you.
    - Express what you are ready to let go of not to excuse the hurt, but to free yourself from carrying it.
    - State your choice to release the emotional hold the situation has had on you.

1. **Afterward, pause for reflection:** Place both letters in front of you. Notice your breath, your body, and your emotions. Ask yourself:
    - How do I feel now compared to before I began?
    - Did I uncover emotions I had not acknowledged?

- Do I feel lighter, softer, more spacious inside?

You might choose to keep these letters as reminders, tear them up as a symbolic release, or burn them safely as an act of letting go.

**Case Study Discussion: Alice's Journey**

Alice had been struggling with love for as long as she could remember. She had been in and out of relationships but never found herself truly happy. At the age of 58, she finally realised that she needed to forgive herself before she could truly love herself and be in a genuine relationship. Alice had always struggled with self–esteem and self–worth, and this had reflected in all of her relationships. She would always put her partners first and often found herself being taken advantage of. It was not until we started journeying together that she realised the root cause of her struggles. Through our sessions together over many months Alice was able to confront the issues that were holding her back and started working on self–forgiveness. She realised that in order to move on and start living a heart–led life, she needed to forgive herself for all the mistakes she had made in the past. With self–forgiveness came self–love, and Alice started to see herself in a new light. She started doing things that made her happy and began to take care of herself. She also started to attract genuine and loving relationships into her life. Alice's journey towards forgiveness was not an easy one, but it was definitely worth it. She realised that forgiveness was not just about letting go of the past but also about accepting herself and loving herself unconditionally. Her heart was finally open to receive and give love, and she began living a more fulfilled life than ever before. Alice's story is a powerful reminder that self–forgiveness is an essential step in living a heart–led life. It is about releasing yourself from the burden of your past mistakes, accepting yourself for who you are, and loving yourself unconditionally.

**Reflective Exercise: Alice's Journey**

Here are four profound and reflective questions inspired by Alice's story to help you engage with your own journey to forgiveness:

**1. What pain have you been carrying that no longer serves your healing?:** *Alice held on to the hurt because she thought releasing it meant the other person won, but in truth, it only kept her stuck. Forgiveness does not erase your experience, it frees you from reliving it.*

**2. If you no longer needed an apology, what could you begin to let go of today?:** *Waiting for an apology kept Alice tied to the past. When she chose to forgive without conditions, she reclaimed her energy and inner peace. You do not need permission to begin healing.*

**3. What would it feel like to forgive yourself for what you did not know then?:** *Alice's greatest act of forgiveness was turning compassion inward. When she stopped blaming herself for how she coped, she softened. Forgiveness opened the door to self-love and wholeness.*

**4. What part of your heart is asking to be heard, not hardened?** *Anger protected Alice for a long time, but underneath it was grief, and beneath that, longing. When she finally listened to her own heart, forgiveness emerged, not as a demand, but as a gentle return to herself.*

**Affirmations For Integration: (Heart Whispers)**

Affirmations have the power to quiet the noise of doubt, open the doorway to self-trust, and draw you back into the wisdom of your heart. When practised daily, they nurture an inner dialogue based in love and truth, helping you live each day more aligned with who you truly are. I invite you to repeat silently or write:

- *I am willing to let go of resentment and anger.*
- *I am open to forgiveness as a healing process.*
- *I choose to release negative emotions and embrace forgiveness.*
- *I accept responsibility for my actions and seek forgiveness.*
- *I am learning to forgive myself and others.*
- *I am grateful for the peace that comes with forgiveness.*
- *I am committed to releasing grudges and embracing forgiveness.*

**Reflective Exercise - Forgiveness Visualisation Walk**

**Step 1 – Prepare:** Choose a quiet path, whether it is through a park, along the beach, or in your neighbourhood, somewhere you can walk without rushing. Before you begin, place your hand over your heart and set the intention: *"I walk to release, to heal, and to move forward."*

**Step 2 - Begin with Breath:** As you start walking, focus on your breathing. Inhale deeply through your nose, drawing in fresh, clean air. Exhale slowly through your mouth, imagining that each breath out carries away a small piece of the pain, resentment, or hurt you have been holding.

**Step 3 - Visualise Release:** With every step, picture your emotional burdens as stones you have been carrying. Feel them grow lighter as they drop, one by one, onto the earth behind you. You might imagine them dissolving into the ground, transformed into something neutral, no longer weighing you down.

**Step 4 - Engage Your Senses:** Notice the warmth or coolness of the air on your skin, the sound of your footsteps, the rustle of leaves, the scent of nature around you. Allow the world to remind you that life is happening now, in this present moment, not in the pain of the past.

**Step 5 - Closing Ritual:** When you reach the end of your walk, stand still. Place your feet firmly on the ground and take three slow, deep breaths. In your final exhale, whisper or say aloud: **"I release the past. I walk forward in peace."**

Take a moment to notice the shift inside you, a little more lightness, a little more space, a little more peace.

### Closing Reflection

Forgiveness is not about forgetting. It is not about making what happened acceptable or pretending it did not hurt. Forgiveness is about **reclaiming your peace**, your energy, and your capacity to love, even in the aftermath of pain. You have travelled through the raw terrain of resentment, grief, anger, and regret. You have sat with truths that were difficult to name, and now, you stand at a threshold, not of erasure, but of release. To forgive is not to condone. It is to choose freedom over fixation. It is to untangle yourself from a story that no longer defines who you are. It is to soften your grip on the past, so your hands can be open to the present, and perhaps most courageously of all, it is to forgive **yourself,** for what you did not know, for how you survived, for being human. Let this be your beginning, not your ending:

***A return to wholeness. A renewal of compassion.***

***A quiet unbinding of the heart.***

***You are not here to be perfect.***

***You are here to be free.***

**The Unbound Journey Belongs to You**

Where you go from here is your choice, but you do not walk alone. The rest of the Unbound Series is there to guide you, and the online programs are there to support you. Choose the next chapter of your becoming – www.timetotransform.world

# MODULE 10 – KINDNESS

## Your Opening Reflection

**Invitation to Kindness** - As you enter this module, I invite you to soften your heart toward yourself. Let go of the urge to strive or judge, and instead welcome the gentleness that kindness offers. Imagine speaking to yourself the way you would to someone you deeply love, with tenderness, patience, and compassion. This is your chance to practice kindness not as a fleeting act, but as a way of being, beginning with how you meet yourself in this very moment.

- "When was the last time you were truly kind to yourself?"
- "What does kindness toward yourself look and feel like in your daily life?"
- "When you think of being kind to others, do you extend the same grace to yourself?"
- "What beliefs or habits sometimes stop you from treating yourself with kindness?"
- "How does your body respond when you speak to yourself with compassion instead of criticism?"
- "If a loved one were in your shoes today, how would you show them kindness, and can you offer that to yourself?"

Let these questions open the doorway into presence. Every answer you give, whether in words, sensations, or silence, is a bridge between where you are and where you are going.

## Learning Objectives

The learning objectives are included here to give you a clear focus for this module, ensuring that each practice you explore moves you closer to mastering the skills, insights, and heart-led awareness that will enrich your life well beyond the program. By the end of this module, you will:

- Understand the emotional and relational impact of kindness on yourself and others.
- Explore the role of kindness in building emotional resilience and connection.
- Practice self-kindness as a foundation for empathy and compassion.
- Identify opportunities to integrate kindness into your everyday choices.
- Recognise kindness as a transformative force for living a heart-led life.

## Core Emotional Domains

The core emotional intelligence domains covered here are essential because they form the foundation for lasting heart connection, guiding you to deepen self-awareness, regulate emotions, build resilience, and strengthen the mind-body bond throughout your *Unbound* journey.

- **Self-Awareness:** Kindness invites you to pause and notice your internal state, your emotions, assumptions, and judgments, so you can choose to respond with intention and care.
- **Empathy:** By practicing kindness, you attune more deeply to the emotions and needs of others, strengthening your ability to connect, listen, and relate with compassion.
- **Self-Regulation:** In moments of tension, kindness helps you shift from reactivity to presence. It softens harsh responses and creates space for grace under pressure.
- **Social Skills:** Kindness enhances your ability to build trust, nurture meaningful relationships, and create emotionally safe environments where others feel seen and valued.
- **Motivation (Intrinsic Growth through Compassion):** When guided by kindness, your growth becomes heart-led. You are motivated not by external rewards, but by the joy of contributing, uplifting, and embodying your values.

### "Kindness – Gentle Strength In Action"

Kindness is more than a moral virtue, it is a transformative emotional intelligence practice that awakens connection, inner strength, and authentic leadership. In today's fast-paced, outcome-driven world, kindness is often misunderstood as soft or passive, but in truth, kindness is courageous. It takes strength to slow down, to listen, and to respond with compassion when reacting with criticism would be easier. It requires emotional maturity to stay grounded in empathy, even when you are under pressure or facing misunderstanding. Kindness begins within. It starts with your willingness to speak gently to yourself, to forgive your own missteps, and to create space for growth without harshness. This inner kindness builds a **healthy, grounded sense of self-worth,** not based on how much you achieve, but on how deeply you honour your own humanity. From that space, kindness naturally extends outward. It becomes the bridge between you and others, enhancing your ability to understand their needs, emotions, and perspectives. You become more attuned in conversation, more responsive in conflict, and more intentional in your presence. This nurtures trust, strengthens relationships, and develops emotional safety, core foundations of **social intelligence**. In leadership, whether you lead a team, a classroom, a family, or your own life, kindness becomes a guiding force. It does not dilute effectiveness; it amplifies it. When you lead with kindness, people feel seen, respected, and inspired. Your influence grows not through control, but through care. Ultimately, kindness is not something you perform. It is something you embody. It shapes how you live, relate, and serve. It invites you to return to the heart again and again, to respond to life not from fear or ego, but from empathy, integrity, and compassion. *Kindness is a practice. Kindness is power. Kindness is the courage to lead, live, and love with humanity.*

### Kindness As An Emotional Regulation Tool

Kindness is not just an outward gesture, it is a powerful internal mechanism for emotional regulation. When you choose to respond with kindness, especially in emotionally charged situations, you activate parts of your brain associated with empathy, connection, and calm. This helps to quiet the amygdala, your brain's threat detector, and reduces the fight, flight, or freeze response that often fuels reactivity, defensiveness, or aggression. When you are overwhelmed or frustrated, pausing to practice kindness, toward yourself or others, creates a physiological and psychological shift. It lowers your cortisol (the stress hormone), slows your heart rate, and brings your nervous system back into balance. This allows you to move from reaction to reflection, from anger to curiosity, from fear to care. Importantly, kindness does not mean ignoring boundaries or denying difficult feelings. Instead, it invites you to meet those emotions with gentleness, compassion, and self-awareness. Whether you are speaking kindly to yourself during moments of shame or extending grace to someone who has hurt you, kindness becomes a choice to stay regulated and present. Over time, using kindness as a regulation tool strengthens your resilience. It builds your inner muscle to stay grounded under pressure, to repair relationships with humility, and to speak truth without harm. It becomes a steady anchor that helps you navigate life with clarity, connection, and emotional maturity. In this way, kindness is not just a reaction, it is a conscious practice of returning to your centre, softening your edges, and choosing the heart over the impulse.

**The Neuroscience Of Kindness: Oxytocin, Serotonin, And Social Bonding**

Kindness does not just feel good, it is wired into your brain and body as a deeply healing and connecting experience. When you offer or receive a kind gesture, a cascade of neurochemical activity is activated that supports emotional wellbeing, resilience, and human connection.

<u>Oxytocin - The *"Connection Hormone"*</u>

Oxytocin is often called the *love* or *bonding hormone.* Acts of kindness, like a warm smile, a thoughtful message, or a compassionate touch, stimulate the release of oxytocin. This hormone promotes trust, emotional openness, and social bonding. It reduces stress, lowers blood pressure, and creates a sense of safety. In both giver and receiver, oxytocin enhances feelings of closeness and belonging, reinforcing positive social behaviours. When you consciously engage in acts of kindness, you are not only nurturing someone else's wellbeing, you are also nourishing your own body and mind at a biological level. Oxytocin does not just make you feel connected, it strengthens your ability to empathise, to listen deeply, and to respond with compassion, even in moments of tension. Over time, these small but powerful hormonal boosts create a feedback loop: the more kindness you give and receive, the more naturally your heart opens, and the more your relationships flourish with trust, warmth, and authenticity.

<u>Serotonin - The Mood Stabiliser</u>

Serotonin plays a key role in regulating your mood, satisfaction, and emotional stability. When you engage in kind, generous behaviour, serotonin levels rise, creating a sense of calm, optimism, and inner balance. Serotonin also contributes to resilience, helping you handle challenges with greater equanimity. Kindness becomes a self-reinforcing practice, boosting your mood while improving your perception of social interactions. As serotonin levels increase, your brain naturally begins to associate kindness with safety and wellbeing, making it more likely that you will repeat those behaviours. Over time, this creates an upward spiral, small acts of kindness not only brighten the moment but also strengthen your long-term emotional stability. By actively cultivating kindness, you are building a mental and emotional foundation that supports patience, perspective, and a steady inner peace, even when external circumstances are uncertain or stressful.

The Kindness Feedback Loop

Neuroscientists have identified a positive feedback loop: when you perform an act of kindness, you feel good, which makes you more likely to be kind again. This cycle builds emotional intelligence, strengthens neural pathways for empathy, and develops long-term wellbeing. Repeated kindness reinforces patterns in the brain that promote connection, trust, and cooperative behaviour. Over time, this feedback loop becomes self-sustaining. The more kindness you practice, the more your brain associates generosity with personal reward and emotional fulfilment. Even small acts, holding a door open, offering a genuine compliment, or listening without judgment, can trigger this cycle. With consistent repetition, your capacity for empathy and compassion deepens, creating a ripple effect that not only enhances your own mental health but also contributes to a more caring and cooperative environment around you.

Kindness and Social Bonding

Humans are social beings, and kindness acts as a bridge between nervous systems. Brain imaging studies show that giving and receiving kindness activates reward centres in the brain, particularly the **ventromedial prefrontal cortex,** an area associated with value-based decisions and social connection. This neurological activity reinforces shared humanity, building stronger personal and community relationships. **In essence**, kindness is not only an emotional or moral virtue, it is a biological imperative. It is a neurochemical strategy for your wellbeing, resilience, and belonging. When you practice kindness regularly, you are not only helping others, you are reshaping your brain, regulating your emotions, and becoming more deeply connected to yourself and the world around you. When you engage in acts of kindness, whether through a simple smile, a listening ear, or a generous act, you are essentially participating in a shared biological dance. Your brain and body synchronise with others in a subtle but profound way, creating a sense of safety and mutual trust. Over time, this builds a reservoir of goodwill that strengthens not only your personal connections but also the collective wellbeing of the groups you belong to. This shared kindness becomes contagious, inspiring others to act with compassion, thus creating a ripple effect that extends far beyond the initial moment of generosity.

### Historical And Spiritual Foundations Of Kindness Across Traditions

Kindness is not a modern invention, it is a timeless principle based deeply in the wisdom traditions, philosophies, and spiritual teachings of cultures across the world. From ancient scriptures to oral traditions, acts of compassion and benevolence have long been recognised as both sacred duty and powerful pathways to personal and collective transformation.

Christianity

In the Christian tradition, kindness is a core fruit of the Spirit (Galatians 5:22–23) and a central commandment. Jesus' teachings consistently emphasise mercy, love for one's neighbour, and forgiveness. The parable of the Good Samaritan embodies kindness beyond boundaries of race or religion, showing that true compassion is unconditional. Christians are taught that to be kind is to reflect the nature of God: "*Be kind and compassionate to one another, forgiving each other, just as in Christ God forgave you*" (Ephesians 4:32).

Hinduism

In Hindu philosophy, kindness is expressed through the principle of **ahimsa**, or non-violence. Based in the Vedas and embraced by sages like Mahatma Gandhi, ahimsa extends beyond refraining from harm to actively choosing compassion in thoughts, words, and deeds. Acts of kindness are seen as expressions of **dharma,** right action, and contribute to the spiritual growth of both giver and receiver.

Buddhism

Buddhist teachings place **metta**, or loving-kindness, at the heart of spiritual practice. Metta meditation involves sending intentions of goodwill to oneself and all beings, even those who are difficult to love. The Buddha taught that cultivating loving-kindness dissolves anger, softens the heart, and leads to liberation from suffering. Kindness is not seen as passive, it is courageous, conscious, and transformative.

Judaism

In Judaism, kindness is a form of **chesed,** a covenantal love and steadfast kindness that mirrors God's relationship with humanity. The Torah is filled with injunctions to care for the widow, the orphan, and the stranger, making kindness a divine command and a social responsibility. The Talmud teaches: "*The world is built on kindness*" (Psalm 89:2), affirming its role in sustaining communities and spiritual life.

Islam

In Islam, kindness is both a spiritual virtue and a daily obligation. The Prophet Muhammad (peace be upon him) said, "*Kindness is a mark of faith, and whoever is not kind has no faith.*" The Qur'an urges believers to respond to evil with good, and to treat others with mercy, even when they differ. Allah is described as **Ar-Rahman, Ar-Rahim,** the Most Compassionate, the Most Merciful, encouraging Muslims to embody divine compassion in all interactions.

Indigenous and Earth-Based Traditions

Across Indigenous cultures, kindness is intimately woven into the fabric of life. It is expressed through **reciprocity,** giving back to the Earth, to the ancestors, and to one's community with humility and gratitude. In many traditions, elders teach that kindness is not optional but essential for harmony and survival. It is a sacred duty to walk gently, speak with care, and uphold the dignity of all beings.

A Shared Moral Thread

Though cultures and languages differ, the essence of kindness remains remarkably universal. Whether called **karuna**, **chesed**, **metta**, or **compassion**, it reflects the deep human understanding that love, empathy, and care are essential for both spiritual growth and societal wellbeing. To live kindly is to participate in the ancient rhythm of humanity, one that honours dignity, connection, and the sacredness of life. When you choose kindness, you are not just following a personal value, you are stepping into a global, intergenerational legacy of healing, hope, and heart.

## Kindness To Others *And* Self As A Path To Wholeness

Kindness is often celebrated as a virtue we extend outward, but its true power lies in its ability to transform us from within. When you choose kindness, not only toward others but also toward yourself, you are actively participating in your own healing and integration. Kindness becomes a bridge, from fragmentation to wholeness, from harshness to harmony.

To Others: Building Bridges of Belonging

When you act kindly toward others, you affirm their worth and humanity. Simple acts, listening deeply, offering help, speaking gently, send the message: *You matter. You are seen.* In a world that often feels disconnected or competitive, kindness restores trust. It creates spaces of psychological safety, encourages cooperation, and strengthens bonds of empathy and belonging. You begin to realise that your kindness is not a gift from a place of superiority, it is a mutual recognition of shared vulnerability, and in that mutual recognition, something powerful happens: you see yourself in the other. Compassion is no longer abstract. It becomes the language of your heart.

To Yourself: Returning to Inner Safety

True wholeness cannot be achieved if you only extend kindness outward while withholding it from yourself. Many of us are our own harshest critics. We replay mistakes, dwell in guilt, or measure ourselves against impossible standards, but when you learn to speak to yourself with gentleness, to say "*It is okay,*" "*I am doing my best,*" or "*I deserve rest*", you shift the entire tone of your inner world. Kindness to self softens inner rigidity. It welcomes your imperfections and reminds you that healing is not linear. It creates space for rest, recovery, and renewal. It is not indulgent, it is intelligent, because when you are kind to yourself, you are more resilient, more present, and more capable of showing up fully for others.

The Healing Synergy

Kindness creates a feedback loop between your self and others. When you offer compassion outward, you are more likely to internalise it. When you nurture yourself, you are more grounded and generous in how you relate to the world. This synergy creates emotional intelligence, relational depth, and a grounded sense of purpose. Wholeness is not about perfection. It is about integration, bringing all parts of yourself, including your wounds, into the light of compassion. Kindness is the light. It does not fix everything instantly, but it melts what is frozen, mends what is torn, and reconnects what has been lost.

## Kindness In High-Performance, High-Pressure Environments

### Kindness Builds Stronger Teams

In high-pressure environments, the temptation to isolate, micromanage, or push harder can backfire. Kindness enables psychological safety, an environment where people feel comfortable expressing concerns, making mistakes, and being human. This is the foundation of high-functioning teams. When kindness is practiced through active listening, genuine recognition, or supportive feedback, teams become more cohesive, adaptive, and innovative. Kindness also develops mutual trust, which strengthens collaboration and reduces conflict. When you lead with empathy and offer encouragement instead of criticism, you invite others to bring their best ideas forward without fear of judgment. This not only boosts morale but also inspires creativity and problem-solving. In moments of stress or uncertainty, your kindness becomes a stabilising force, reminding your team that they are valued as people, not just as performers. Over time, this builds a resilient, connected culture where everyone feels invested in shared success.

### Kindness to Self: Preventing Burnout

High achievers often extend compassion to others but struggle to show it to themselves. Overwork becomes a badge of honour, and self-kindness is mistaken for weakness. Yet, research consistently shows that self-compassion enhances motivation, perseverance, and wellbeing. In high-stakes roles, self-kindness is not a luxury, it is a lifeline. When you treat yourself with understanding rather than criticism during times of failure or fatigue, you recover faster and return stronger. By practicing kindness toward yourself, you build an inner foundation that can weather pressure without collapsing. You give yourself permission to rest, recharge, and reflect without guilt, allowing your mind and body to heal. This compassionate self-awareness helps you sustain your passion, sharpen your focus, and approach challenges with clarity instead of depletion. When you honour your own needs, you are not only preserving your energy, you are also modelling to others that resilience is built through care, not constant strain.

### Kindness as a Leadership Imperative

Great leaders do not just demand results, they create conditions where people thrive. Kindness in leadership is not about being permissive or avoiding hard conversations. It is about delivering truth with humanity, making decisions with integrity, and recognising the inherent dignity in every team member. In the long run, kindness sustains performance by fuelling loyalty, engagement, and purpose. In high-performance environments, kindness is not an afterthought or a sign of weakness. It is a conscious choice that strengthens culture, enhances outcomes, and builds resilient, emotionally intelligent people. ***When pressure rises, let kindness lead. It is both your edge and your anchor.*** When you embody kindness as a leader, you set a tone that ripples through the entire organisation. Your example invites openness, develops mutual respect, and encourages others to step into their best selves. You create a climate where people feel valued for more than just their output, and as a result, they give more of themselves, not out of fear or obligation, but out of genuine commitment. This type of leadership does not just achieve short-term goals; it nurtures long-term growth, trust, and loyalty that endure far beyond any single project or performance review.

**Forgiveness Exercise: *"The Mirror of Gentle Words"***

**Purpose:** To cultivate self-kindness and rewire the internal dialogue through embodied practice, this gentle exercise helps you see yourself with compassion and speak to yourself as a trusted friend would.

**Step 1: *Speak 3 Kind Truths Aloud (2 minutes)***

Say three heartfelt affirmations to yourself, slowly and aloud. Choose from these or create your own:

- *"I am learning to love myself."*
- *"I am doing the best I can, and that is enough."*
- *"I deserve kindness, especially from myself."*

Let your words settle into your heart. If emotions rise, allow them to move through you gently.

**Step 2: *Write a Letter to Yourself (5 minutes)***

Using a journal, write a short note to yourself as if you were writing to someone you deeply care about. Start with:

*"Dear [Your Name], I want you to know…"*

Let kindness guide your pen. No need to fix or change anything, just witness yourself with love.

**Integration Reflection**

Kindness to yourself is not indulgence, it is nourishment. This practice grounds you in compassion and begins to replace old inner criticism with acceptance and truth. Repeat this ritual as needed, especially on days when your heart feels tender or unseen.

**Case Study Discussion: Isabella's Journey**

Isabella was always there for others. She was the first to offer help and the last to leave when someone needed her. She was kind, compassionate and caring, but she had a hard time showing that same kindness to herself. Isabella self–talk was brutal, constantly telling herself that she was not good enough, smart enough or pretty enough. Isabella felt that she was not worthy and did not deserve kindness or love from herself or anyone. Over time in our sessions, Isabella realised that she could not keep giving to others if she did not give to herself. She started by practicing self–compassion and self–care. She began to treat herself with the same kindness and respect she showed to others. It was not easy for her at first, but with practice, she started to change the way she talked to herself and the way she treated herself._ As Isabella's heart opened up to kindness, she began to see and feel into herself differently. She started to believe that she was lovable, just as she was. Isabella discovered that showing herself kindness allowed her to be more patient, understanding, and accepting of others. Her relationships with her family and friends deepened, and she felt more connected to the people around her. Isabella learned that kindness started with herself. She had to be kind to herself before she could be truly kind to others. She realised that she had to fill her own cup before she could pour into others. By gifting kindness to herself, Isabella was able to live a more heart–led life, where love and compassion flowed freely. Today, Isabella continues to practice self–kindness and uses her experience to help others who may be struggling with the same issues she once faced. She knows that living a heart–led life means being kind to yourself and others, and that kindness is the key to unlocking a life full of love and joy.

**Reflective Exercise: Isabella's Journey**

Here are four profound and reflective questions inspired by Isabella's story to help you engage with your own kindness journey:

1. **What would change if you spoke to yourself with the same compassion you offer others?** *Reflection:* You often give others grace, comfort, and encouragement, but what if you gave that same gift to yourself? Your inner voice shapes your emotional landscape. When you soften it with kindness, you create space for healing, growth, and joy. You become your own ally, not your harshest critic.
2. **When was the last time you truly acknowledged your own worth?** *Reflection:* Worthiness is not something you earn, it is something you already possess. Like Isabella, you may have learned to be kind to others while overlooking yourself, but you deserve love, rest, and recognition. Your value is not conditional. Begin by honouring yourself, gently and consistently.
3. **In what ways has withholding kindness from yourself affected your ability to give it freely to others?** *Reflection:* You cannot pour from an empty cup. If your self-kindness is lacking, giving to others may start to feel exhausting or transactional, but when you fill your heart with compassion for yourself, you do not run dry you overflow. True kindness is sustainable when it starts within.
4. **What daily ritual could help you nurture self-kindness as a way of life?** *Reflection:* Self-kindness does not require grand gestures, it lives in your small, intentional choices: how you speak to yourself in the mirror, how you rest, how you forgive your mistakes.

Start simple. Let kindness become a habit, a rhythm, a sacred return to your heart each day.

***These questions and reflections are designed to gently guide you inward, to recognise that kindness is not only what you give, but also what you allow yourself to receive. Like Isabella, you too can open your heart to yourself and live more freely, more fully, and more compassionately.***

**Affirmations For Integration: (Heart Whispers)**

Affirmations have the power to quiet the noise of doubt, open the doorway to self-trust, and draw you back into the wisdom of your heart. When practised daily, they nurture an inner dialogue based in love and truth, helping you live each day more aligned with who you truly are. I invite you to repeat silently or write:

- *I show kindness to everyone I meet.*
- *I believe in the power of kindness.*
- *I feel happy when I show kindness to others.*
- *I practice self–kindness every day.*
- *I believe that kindness can change the world.*
- *I feel grateful for acts of kindness shown to me.*
- *I choose kindness even in challenging situations.*
- *I create a ripple of kindness wherever I go.*

**The Kindness Ripple Exercise:**

I invite you to commit to one small act of kindness for yourself and one for someone else over the next 24 hours. Write it down, reflect on intention, and share with a partner if comfortable. Example acts:

- Writing a forgiveness letter to yourself
- Paying for someone's coffee
- Setting a firm but loving boundary
- Saying something kind to yourself in the mirror

When you consciously choose and act on kindness, you plant a seed that can grow far beyond the moment. The person you help may go on to help someone else, and the kindness you show yourself may inspire deeper self-respect and healthier boundaries in the days ahead. In this way, even the smallest gesture can ripple through lives, touching people you may never meet and creating waves of compassion that extend far beyond your immediate circle.

**Closing Reflection**

In a world that often glorifies speed, achievement, and self-interest, your choice to slow down and lead with compassion is not just countercultural, it is a profound act of strength. It is the decision to be a source of light in a landscape that can sometimes feel cold and unyielding. Today, as you have reflected on kindness, toward others and, perhaps most importantly, toward yourself, remember this: the gentleness you offer yourself becomes fertile soil. From that soil, your empathy blossoms, your patience deepens, and your courage takes root. This is where true resilience grows, not in the relentless pushing, but in the tender tending of your own heart. When you choose to soften instead of harde. When you speak to yourself with care instead of criticis. When you see others not as threats, but as fellow humans doing their best. You create ripples of healing, connection, and peace, not just for others, but for yourself. Kindness is not a task to check off; it is a way of moving through the world. Carry it forward as a steady rhythm in your words, in your actions, in your pauses, and in your presence. Let kindness shape your relationships, your work, and the way you see the world. Let kindness be your anchor in storms and your light in darkness. Let it be the language your heart speaks, in quiet moments, in challenging moments, in every moment, to every soul you meet, including your own, and as you live this way, you may discover something extraordinary: kindness not only changes the lives it touches, it transforms the one who gives it most of all.

**There Is More in You Than You Know**

This module has revealed a glimpse of your inner strength, and there is more to be found. The rest of the Unbound Series will help you uncover it, one courageous step at a time – **www.timetotransform.world**

# MODULE 11 – REFLECTION

**Your Opening Reflection**

**Invitation to Pause and Honour Your Journey -** As you arrive in this module, I invite you to pause and recognise the courage it took to walk this far. Reflection is not about measuring progress, but about listening to the quiet truths your heart has revealed along the way. Every moment of insight, every breath of stillness, every tear or smile has been a step home to yourself. Allow this space to become a mirror, showing you how far you have come and how deeply you have grown. Honour your journey, not for its perfection, but for its honesty, resilience, and love.

- "What has shifted in your heart over this journey?"
- "What is one moment that you will carry with you forever?"
- "Which practice, teaching, or moment felt most alive for you, and why?"
- "Where in your life do you now feel a greater sense of freedom, clarity, or belonging?"
- "What part of yourself have you reconnected with or rediscovered along the way?"
- "If your heart could speak one truth from this journey, what would it say?"

Let these questions open the doorway into presence. Every answer you give, whether in words, sensations, or silence, is a bridge between where you are and where you are going.

**Learning Objectives**

The learning objectives are included here to give you a clear focus for this module, ensuring that each practice you explore moves you closer to mastering the skills, insights, and heart-led awareness that will enrich your life well beyond the program. By the end of this module, you will:

- Develop emotional intelligence through structured self-reflection
- Honour personal growth, insights, and transformation from the 28-day journey
- Learn to integrate heart-centred practices into everyday life
- Set heart-led intentions for future emotional development and authentic living

**Core Emotional Domains**

The core emotional intelligence domains covered here are essential because they form the foundation for lasting heart connection, guiding you to deepen self-awareness, regulate emotions, build resilience, and strengthen the mind-body bond throughout your *Unbound* journey.

- **Self-Awareness:** Reflection begins with noticing what has shifted within you. You become more attuned to your thoughts, emotions, and patterns, gaining insight into how you have grown and where you still hold resistance. This self-awareness helps you recognise your journey with clarity and compassion, not judgment.
- **Self-Reflection:** Taking time to pause and look inward allows you to make sense of your experiences. You begin to connect the dots, between your past and present, your choices and values. Through reflection, you learn to hold space for both your breakthroughs and your imperfections with honesty and grace.
- **Emotional Integration:** Emotions are not meant to be isolated or buried, they are meant to be understood and integrated. Reflection helps you acknowledge the full spectrum of what you have felt and lived. By weaving these emotional threads together, you create coherence within yourself and grow into greater wholeness.
- **Empathy and Compassion:** As you reflect on your own journey, you naturally open to the experiences of others. You begin to see that everyone is carrying their own story, their own struggles and triumphs.

This awareness cultivates empathy and deepens your ability to meet both yourself and others with kindness.

- **Purpose and Values Alignment:** Reflection brings you back to what matters most. It realigns you with your inner compass, your values, your purpose, your truth. From this place of alignment, you can move forward with greater intention, choosing a path that honours both who you are and who you are becoming.

**"Reflection – Integrating, Honouring, And Continuing Your Heart Journey"**

Reflection is the final module of any meaningful journey, and the first page of the next. It is the sacred pause that allows you to breathe, integrate, and truly see how far you have come. Without reflection, even the most powerful experiences can pass unnoticed. However, when you take the time to look inward with honesty and compassion, experience transforms into wisdom, and moments become milestones. Reflection strengthens your **emotional intelligence** by inviting you to move beyond reaction into conscious understanding. It helps you trace the emotional patterns that shaped your choices, the shifts in your self-awareness, and the quiet inner awakenings that have taken root along the way. Through this process, you begin to internalise the growth you have undergone, not just as something you *did*, but as something you have *become*. In reflection, you give your heart a voice. You listen not only to what happened, but to what it meant. You begin to see your resilience, your courage, your tenderness, and your truth. You allow yourself to feel gratitude, grieve what's been released, and honour the parts of you that stepped forward in new ways, and most importantly, you use that insight to set **aligned intentions,** intentions that do not come from pressure or fear, but from clarity and purpose. These are heart-led intentions that help you move forward in a way that feels true to who you are now, not who you used to be. Reflection is not just about looking back. It is about looking within, and from there, stepping into the next chapter with grounded wisdom, emotional depth, and an open heart. This is the moment where your journey becomes part of you, woven into your being, carried forward not as memory, but as transformation.

**The Neuroscience Of Reflection: How Pausing Strengthens Neural Integration**

In a world that urges you to keep moving, stay productive, and push forward, choosing to pause might feel uncomfortable, or even unnecessary. However, neuroscience, like your heart, knows the truth: **reflection is not a luxury, it is a biological and emotional necessity.** When you pause to reflect, you are not just thinking about your experiences, you are changing your brain. You are helping it integrate the stories you have lived, the emotions you have felt, and the growth you have undergone. This process is called **neural integration**, and it is essential for lasting healing and transformation.

<u>What is Happening in Your Brain When You Reflect?</u>

When you pause to reflect, powerful processes unfold within your brain. You engage the **prefrontal cortex**, the region responsible for self-awareness, emotional regulation, empathy, and future planning. This is where you begin to step outside of autopilot, observing your thoughts and feelings instead of being ruled by them. Reflection strengthens your ability to choose how you respond, rather than being swept away by old patterns. At the same time, the **default mode network (DMN)** becomes active. This interconnected system allows you to revisit memories, explore meaning, and imagine new possibilities. It is here that your brain weaves together past experiences with present insight, helping you see connections that may have been hidden in the busyness of daily life. When you reflect, your brain is literally rewiring itself. Neural pathways associated with mindfulness, compassion, and perspective-taking grow stronger. Stress pathways begin to quiet, and your ability to regulate emotions improves. Over time, this repeated practice builds resilience, clarity, and wisdom. In essence, reflection allows your brain to integrate experience into understanding. You begin to link what you have felt with what you have learned, bridging the gap between who you once were and who you are becoming. This is not just a mental process, it is the deepening of your emotional intelligence. You are learning to respond with clarity, compassion, and intention, instead of reacting from fear or habit. Reflection is where growth takes root. It is where insight turns into transformation, and where the wisdom of your journey becomes part of the person you are choosing to be.

<u>Creating Coherence: The Power of Neural Integration</u>

Throughout this journey, you have lived many different moments, some filled with joy, some marked by pain, and others still unfolding in quiet ways. Left unexamined, these experiences can remain fragmented, scattered across your inner landscape like unconnected puzzle pieces. Reflection is the practice that gathers them together, weaving them into a meaningful whole. When you pause to reflect, you bring your **thoughts, feelings, memories, and insights into alignment**. This process is known as **neural integration**, the harmonising of different parts of your brain so that your inner world becomes coherent rather than chaotic. Instead of being pulled in many directions by conflicting emotions or scattered memories, you begin to see the larger picture of your own growth. Neuroscience shows that integration strengthens the connections between your prefrontal cortex (awareness and regulation), your limbic system (emotions and memory), and your body's felt sense of experience. This creates a state of **coherence**, where your mind, heart, and body work in synergy rather than opposition. The result is not only greater clarity but also greater resilience, you can hold complexity without being overwhelmed. Through reflection, your story shifts from a collection of isolated events to a narrative infused with **meaning and wisdom**. You begin to see patterns, lessons, and truths that may have been hidden in the noise. This understanding deepens your self-trust: you recognise that even the painful moments have shaped you, and that every step has been part of your becoming. Coherence is not about perfection; it is about wholeness. It is about allowing all parts of your experience, light and shadow, triumph and struggle to belong, and to find their place within the larger mosaic of your life. When you practice reflection, you give yourself the gift of integration. From this grounded sense of wholeness, you can move forward with greater compassion, stability, and courage.

<u>What Happens When You Pause?</u>

When you pause, even for a few breaths, you create a profound shift within your body and mind. Instead of running on autopilot or being carried by stress and distraction, your nervous system gently transitions into its **parasympathetic state**, the *"rest-and-digest"* response. This is the physiological space of **calm, safety, and restoration.** In this state, your heart rate slows and steadies, your muscles release tension, and your breath naturally deepens. These simple yet powerful changes signal to your body that you are safe, allowing your mind to soften its grip on survival mode. As your inner world quiets, your brain becomes more receptive to insight, creativity, and self-awareness. Science shows that during a pause, the **coherence between your heart and brain increases**. Instead of operating in conflict, these two powerful centres of intelligence begin to synchronise. Your heart sends signals of steadiness to your brain, helping you regulate emotions, while your brain supports clear thinking and balanced perspective. You literally become more attuned, able to listen with compassion, feel with clarity, and think with presence. Pausing also allows your **default mode network**, the part of the brain responsible for reflection, self-understanding, and meaning-making, to gently awaken. This is why moments of silence often bring sudden clarity, creative ideas, or the memory of something important you had overlooked. On a deeper level, pausing is an act of alignment. It reconnects you to the present moment, where your body, mind, and spirit can finally work together rather than pulling in different directions. You become more grounded in your truth, more open to possibility, and more aligned with your heart's quiet wisdom. The pause does not need to be long, a single mindful breath can be enough to shift you from reactivity into awareness. Over time, the more you practice pausing, the more you train your nervous system to find safety, your mind to find clarity, and your heart to find presence.

<u>You Are the Integration</u>

Reflection is not just something you practice, it is something you embody. It is not an activity separate from your life, but the very process through which you become who you truly are. Reflection is the meeting point of your **emotional growth and neurological transformation**, where your experiences, insights, and feelings weave themselves into wisdom. When you pause and reflect, you create the conditions for integration. You are not merely collecting lessons, you are allowing them to sink deeper, to shape the way you see yourself and the way you show up in the world. Every insight, every tear, every moment of joy becomes a thread, woven into the fabric of your becoming. Reflection is how you turn experiences into meaning, challenges into resilience, and knowledge into embodied truth. So, the next time you feel the urge to keep pushing forward, chasing the next goal or rushing through the moment, remember this: **the pause is powerful**. Growth does not only happen in action; it blossoms in stillness. It is in the quiet spaces of reflection that your transformation takes root.

- **In the stillness, you are healing.** Your nervous system recalibrates, your emotions soften, and your body remembers safety.
- **In the reflection, you are rewiring.** Your brain forms new pathways of clarity, resilience, and compassion.

- **In the awareness, you are becoming whole.** You no longer split yourself between past and future, doubt and desire, you come home to the present, to yourself.

Integration is not a final destination but a way of living. It is the art of carrying your lessons into each breath, each choice, each connection. This is how your heart becomes unbound, not in grand gestures, but in simple, steady moments of return. One breath. One insight. One pause at a time.

**Reflection As A Tool For Long-Term Emotional Growth And Heart-Led Decision-Making**

Reflection is not simply a backward glance, it is a powerful tool that shapes your future. When you take time to pause and reflect, you do more than revisit your experiences, you activate your inner wisdom. You begin to see your journey through the lens of growth, not just memory, and that shift is what transforms reflection into a lifelong resource for emotional intelligence and heart-led living.

Emotional Growth Through Honest Reflection

Every emotional experience you have, joy, sorrow, fear, excitement, carries within it a lesson, a message, a whisper from your heart, but these insights often go unnoticed in the busyness of your life. Reflection gives you the space to return, to feel, to understand. It invites you to explore not just *what happened*, but *how it shaped you*. Through regular, compassionate reflection, you begin to identify your emotional patterns: how you respond under pressure, what triggers your inner critic, where your wounds still ache, and what opens your heart. This awareness does not come from judging yourself, it comes from witnessing yourself with honesty and care. This is how emotional maturity is born, not by avoiding your feelings, but by understanding them and choosing to grow from them. Over time, this process strengthens your emotional resilience, your capacity for empathy, and your ability to meet life with grace rather than reactivity. Your heart becomes wiser, your responses more intentional, and your self-trust more deeply grounded.

Heart-Led Decision-Making Begins with Inner Clarity

When you reflect with presence and purpose, you begin to align your decisions not with fear or habit, but with your **core values**, your **authentic self**, and the quiet knowing of your heart. This is the essence of heart-led decision-making: choosing based on what feels true, not just what seems expected. Reflection helps you ask the deeper questions:

- *Is this choice in alignment with who I am becoming?*
- *Am I acting from fear or from freedom?*
- *Will this decision bring me closer to the life I want to live?*

These questions guide you away from autopilot and toward **conscious, values-based action**. They help you make decisions that nourish your emotional wellbeing and deepen your integrity, not just in moments of ease, but in times of challenge and change. When you learn to trust the wisdom that arises in reflection, you begin to lead your life from within. Your choices become anchored, not just reactive. Your direction becomes heart-led, not externally driven.

<u>Reflection Is the Bridge</u>

Reflection is the bridge between your past and your potential. It is where healing becomes growth, where insight becomes action, and where experience becomes wisdom. The more you return to yourself through reflection, the more empowered and aligned your life becomes. Let reflection be your quiet superpower, the space where you meet yourself honestly, listen deeply, and choose your next step not from pressure, but from purpose. *This is how you become emotionally free. This is how your heart becomes your compass. This is how you live, not just wisely, but fully.*

## Differentiating Rumination From Healthy Contemplation

Reflection is one of the most powerful tools you have for emotional healing and growth, but not all forms of looking inward are helpful. To truly free your heart, it is important to recognise the difference between **rumination** and **healthy contemplation**. While both involve thinking about your experiences, only one leads to peace, insight, and transformation.

<u>What Happens When You Ruminate?</u>

When you ruminate, your thoughts loop in circles. You replay events, question yourself endlessly, or fixate on what went wrong. Rumination tends to be:

- Harsh, self-critical, or full of regret
- Focused on the past without direction
- Driven by fear, guilt, or anxiety

- Emotionally draining and stuck

In this state, you are not learning from the past, you are reliving it. Rumination keeps you emotionally stuck, reinforcing patterns of self-doubt and often worsening your mental and physical wellbeing. It feels heavy, stagnant, and closed.

What Does Healthy Contemplation Look Like?

When you engage in healthy contemplation, you reflect with purpose and compassion. You ask gentle, curious questions like:

- *What am I learning about myself through this?*
- *How did this moment shape me?*
- *What do I need to release or forgive?*

Contemplation invites you to notice without judgment. You begin to understand, integrate, and honour your emotional truth. You give space to both pain and growth, and from that space, you create meaningful direction forward. Contemplation brings movement. It opens your heart, rather than closing it down.

Why This Matters on Your *Unbound Lawyer* Journey

Throughout this program, you have touched many deep and tender parts of yourself. You have remembered, released, and awakened, but now, in reflection, you are invited to tread gently. How you look back matters as much as what you look back on. Reflection can be a doorway to wisdom or a trap of self-criticism. The difference lies in the posture of your heart. When you choose to look back with compassion instead of judgment, you begin to see your journey not as a series of flaws or mistakes, but as the sacred unfolding of becoming. Every choice, even the ones you wish had been different, carries a lesson that has shaped your growth. Every moment of vulnerability has been an initiation into greater strength and authenticity. Reflection, then, is not about perfecting your past but about honouring the wisdom it has given you. This is the heart's invitation: to release the loop of rumination and step into the clarity of contemplation. Rumination keeps you circling the same pain, replaying the same doubts. Contemplation, on the other hand, invites you to pause, listen, and ask, *What is this moment here to teach me?* In doing so, you transform memory into meaning and struggle into strength. By reflecting in this way, you give yourself the gift of emotional freedom. The past no longer defines you, it informs you. You learn to carry its lessons lightly, with grace, allowing them to guide rather than weigh you down. In this process, trust in your inner wisdom deepens. You begin to see that your heart has always been whispering the way forward, and that whisper becomes your compass. This is why reflection matters. It anchors your transformation. It helps you embody your insights, integrate your healing, and align with the deepest truth of who you are. In choosing reflection over rumination, you step into the freedom of living from your heart, not your history.

A Gentle Check-In

The next time your thoughts pull you into the past, pause and ask yourself: ***"Am I looping, or am I listening?"*** If you are looping, soften. If you are listening, keep going, with kindness. Let your reflection be a safe space, not a battleground. This is how your heart becomes unbound, not by repeating the pain, but by meeting it with understanding and choosing to grow from it.

**Integrating Past Lessons To Build Future Resilience**

Resilience does not mean you have never been hurt. It means you have allowed your pain to teach you something, and you have chosen to grow from it. As you reach this final stage of the *Unbound Lawyer* journey, you are invited to reflect not just on what you have been through, but on **how you have emerged**. The process of *integration* is what transforms experience into strength, and memory into wisdom. You have faced emotions, truths, and turning points, some of them uncomfortable, all of them meaningful, but reflection is what allows you to hold these moments in your hands and ask, *"What did this teach me? Who have I become because of it?"* This is how you build resilience, not by forgetting the past, but by **weaving it into your foundation**.

Why Integration Matters

There have been moments when you felt heavy with uncertainty, weighed down by doubt, or caught in the tangle of old patterns, and there have also been moments when your heart lifted, when your breath deepened, when you touched a strength or softness within you that surprised you. Both are part of your journey. Both hold meaning. If you rush past these experiences, they scatter like fragments of a story left unfinished. They remain unanchored, unable to guide or sustain you, but when you pause to reflect, something powerful begins to happen: the fragments start to form a whole. You begin to notice the threads that connect your pain to your healing, your challenges to your growth, your fears to your courage. Integration is not about erasing the past or fixing every wound. It is about honouring what has been, reclaiming the lessons, and recognising that nothing was wasted. The heartbreaks, the breakthroughs, the struggles, and the joys all become woven into a tapestry that tells the truth of who you are becoming. To integrate is to gather your pieces and place them gently where they belong, not tucked away in shame or regret, but honoured as part of your strength. It is the process of seeing yourself clearly, of realising that your journey has shaped you in ways that are both tender and resilient. When you integrate, you no longer live in fragments. You stand whole. You carry your past not as a burden, but as a foundation. You live with greater clarity, steadiness, and compassion for yourself and others. Integration matters because it transforms experience into wisdom, wounds into gifts, and moments into meaning.

Resilience as a Heart-Led Practice

When you integrate your lessons, you do more than remember, you strengthen the foundation of your being. Each reflection becomes a brick laid with intention, building a steadiness that holds you even in life's storms. You begin to trust that no matter what unfolds, you have the capacity to move through it. Why? Because you already have. You have faced challenges, felt the ache of uncertainty, and still found a way forward. That memory lives in your heart as evidence of your strength. True resilience is not about armouring yourself or hardening against life. It is not the absence of pain, but the presence of trust. It is a soft, steady knowing that you are capable of meeting what comes with awareness, grace, and compassion. This heart-led resilience does not reject struggle, it recognises it as part of the path. Every challenge becomes an invitation to return to your breath, your truth, and your deeper self. With each cycle of falling and rising, reflecting and realigning, you expand your inner capacity. You begin to see your past not as a series of wounds that broke you, but as experiences that shaped and built you. What once felt heavy becomes a teacher. What once felt overwhelming becomes a reminder of how far you have come. Resilience, then, is not just survival, it is transformation. It is the gentle, powerful truth that you are not defined by what happened to you, but by how you continue to meet life with heart.

From Reflection to Future Readiness

When you pause to reflect, you are not only honouring your past, you are preparing your future. Each moment of awareness plants a seed for the life you are still creating. The insights you have gathered, the emotions you have navigated, and the truths you have reclaimed now become guiding lights for the path ahead. Reflection transforms what once felt heavy into wisdom you can carry with strength and grace. As you carry these lessons forward, you begin to make more grounded, heart-aligned choices. You recognise the difference between a reaction based in fear and a response anchored in clarity. Old patterns lose their hold because you have taken the time to understand their roots, and in that understanding, you free yourself from repeating them. Future readiness does not mean predicting or controlling what comes, it means cultivating the inner stability to meet whatever arises. You begin to live from trust: trust in yourself, trust in your resilience, trust in the wisdom of your journey. Decisions flow not from urgency or doubt, but from alignment with your deepest values. This is what long-term emotional resilience looks like: a life guided by reflection, not reaction. It is the quiet confidence that you can move through change without losing yourself. It is the freedom to create your future with intention rather than habit, and it is the courage to step forward knowing that your heart already carries everything you need.

Your Journey Is Your Strength

Everything you have experienced, every stumble, every breakthrough, every tender or painful moment, has shaped you into who you are today. Yet it is not the challenges alone that define you, but the way you have chosen to meet them. It is your willingness to reflect, to integrate, and to grow that transforms life's raw material into wisdom. This is where your true resilience is born. Your strength does not come from having an easy path. It comes from the moments when you were tested and still chose to rise. It comes from the courage to soften instead of harden, to seek understanding instead of shutting down, to open your heart even when fear told you to close it. These choices, repeated again and again, are what make you whole. Let this be your reminder: you are not defined by what you have gone through. You are defined by how you have carried those experiences, how you have learned from them, and how you have allowed them to shape a deeper compassion within you. The scars you carry are not signs of weakness but symbols of strength, evidence that you have endured, healed, and kept moving forward. This is how your heart becomes unbound: not because it has never broken, but because it has been pieced back together with wisdom, truth, and love.

Every fracture has become a window for light. Every loss has made space for growth. Every moment of reflection has pulled you closer to your authentic self. Your journey is not just a story of survival, it is a story of transformation, and as you step forward, you carry within you the undeniable truth: **you are strong, not in spite of your journey, but because of it.**

**Gratitude And Forward-Vision As Tools For Inner Alignment**

Gratitude and forward-vision are more than feel-good practices, they are powerful tools for aligning with your heart's truth. Together, they help you close the chapter behind you with grace and open the one ahead with purpose. Gratitude anchors you in the present, while forward-vision calls you toward your next becoming. When used together, they create a bridge between where you have been and where you are ready to go. This is inner alignment: the state where your emotions, values, choices, and direction are all moving in the same rhythm, **the rhythm of your heart.**

<u>Gratitude Grounds You in Truth</u>

Gratitude is not about ignoring your pain or pretending everything has been easy. It is about choosing to acknowledge the gifts within the journey, *especially* the unexpected ones. When you pause to name what you are grateful for, even in the midst of uncertainty or challenge, you activate a shift in perspective. Gratitude reminds you of your growth. It reconnects you with the people, moments, lessons, and even struggles that shaped your becoming. It turns experience into meaning and scarcity into sufficiency. When you thank the path you have walked, you create the emotional space to move forward without resentment or regret.

<u>Forward-Vision Awakens Possibility</u>

Once you have honoured what has been, you are more open to imagining what could be. Forward-vision invites you to dream beyond your past limitations, to see with the eyes of your heart, not your fear. It is the act of asking, *"What kind of life do I want to live now? Who am I ready to become?"* This visioning is not about rigid goal-setting or chasing perfection. It is about clarity. It is about listening inward and aligning with the values that matter most to you. Forward-vision helps you make choices not out of obligation, but out of alignment, with your purpose, your healing, and your inner truth.

<u>Your Journey Is Your Strength</u>

Everything you have experienced, every stumble, every breakthrough, every tender moment, has shaped you, but it is your willingness to reflect, to integrate, and to *grow from it all* that unlocks your true resilience. Let this be your reminder: you are not defined by what you have gone through. You are defined by what you have *learned*, *integrated*, and *risen from*. This is how your heart becomes unbound, stronger not because it has never broken, but because it has been pieced back together with wisdom, truth, and love.

When Gratitude Meets Vision, You Realign With Your Heart

Gratitude without vision can keep you stuck in comfort. Vision without gratitude can leave you restless and unsatisfied, but when you bring the two together, you create powerful alignment: You recognise the sacredness of where you have been.

- You honour who you are now.
- And you choose where you are going, with intention, not reaction.
- This is what it means to live *from the heart*. You stop running from the past or racing toward the future. Instead, you *align*, step by step, with a life that reflects your wholeness.

Let Gratitude and Vision Guide You Forward

As you complete this stage of your *Unbound* journey, let gratitude be your foundation and vision your guide. Look back with tenderness. Look forward with trust, and in between, return to your breath, your truth, your heart. *You do not need to have all the answers. You just need to stay aligned with what matters. Let that be enough to take the next step.* This is how you walk forward, grateful for the past, open to the future, and fully alive in the now. This is how your heart stays unbound.

**"Mirror of the Heart" Reflection Meditation (Guided Practice)**

I invite you to listen to the Reflection meditation and as you listen to the meditation I would ask you to revisit one moment from this program where you felt the light, your heart felt most open, connected, or free.

**Reflection After Meditation:**

- What emotions arose as you revisited that moment of openness and freedom?
- How does your body respond when you hold that memory in your awareness right now?

- What gentle reminder can you carry with you to return to this feeling when life becomes heavy?
- What did that moment teach you?
- How will you protect and grow that light moving forward?

**Integration Exercise – Heart Anchoring**

After the meditation, place both hands over your heart. Take three slow breaths, and on each inhale, silently repeat: *"I welcome this light."* On each exhale, silently repeat: *"I release what dims it."*

Then, write down one word or phrase that captures the essence of that moment of light (e.g., *peace, belonging, joy, courage*).

Keep this word somewhere visible, on a card, a journal page, or your phone, as an anchor to return to when you need to remember your heart's freedom.

**Case Study Discussion: Nathan's Journey**

***(The following is a transcript of a conversation I (Dr John McSwiney) had with Nathan.)***

"Heart Unbound: The Ultimate 28–Day Heart Connection Challenge' is a significant chapter in my life's story. Prior to this journey, it is fair to say that I was a stranger to my own heart. The first day of the challenge, I was skeptical. Could connecting with my heart really change my life? The first day of the challenge was a revelation. I was guided to close my eyes, take a deep breath, and listen to the whispers of my heart. It was a simple act, but it felt like the start of an extraordinary voyage. Each day, I delved deeper into the program's practices, exploring the uncharted territories of my emotions. I committed to the daily practices and something remarkable started happening. Breathing exercises helped me relax, reducing stress and bringing peace. With every guided meditation, I felt more in tune with my emotions and began to understand the power of vulnerability. Days turned into weeks, and I found myself expressing empathy, forging deeper connections with friends and family. The newfound creativity I discovered astonished me. It was not just a program; it was a profound journey of self–discovery. I was a pragmatist, a workaholic who rarely paused to reflect on my inner self. Stress and deadlines ruled my existence, leaving little room for emotions or personal growth. Through the soothing meditations and introspective exercises, I learned to embrace my vulnerability and connect with my true self. I began to understand that strength lay not in suppressing my emotions but in acknowledging them. With time, I found myself extending this understanding to others, forging profound connections and nurturing empathy in my relationships. As the 28–day challenge drew to a close, I marveled at the person I was changing into. I had transformed from a stoic corporate machine into someone who embraced life's complexities, cherished relationships, and reveled in the beauty of the present moment. 'Heart Unbound' showed me how to unlock my heart's potential, making me a more authentic and fulfilled version of myself. I couldn't help but smile, knowing that this program had changed my life in ways I could never have imagined. The 28–day challenge concluded, but its impact endures. I wake each morning with a heart that beats in harmony with my deepest desires. I have unearthed a wellspring of creativity that colours my world with beauty and purpose. I have grown from a closed–off soul into an authentic, open–hearted individual who revels in life's intricacies. I have spent time with Dr John and have learned to go deeper into my heart and have realised that this is a lifestyle choice, and it is one that I have loved embracing. I would encourage anybody reading this to really embrace this journey because it will change your life.

**Reflection Exercise: Nathan's Journey**

Here are four profound and reflective questions inspired by Nathan's story to help you engage with your own journey of reflection:

1. **In what ways have you come home to yourself during this journey, and how has connecting with your heart shifted the way you see your life, relationships, or purpose?** Like Nathan, you may have begun this journey uncertain or guarded, how has your heart responded as you have opened it day by day?
2. **What past version of yourself do you now hold with greater understanding or compassion, and what strengths have emerged as you have embraced vulnerability and self-awareness?** Consider how your emotional landscape has evolved. Where have you softened? Where have you grown stronger?
3. **What moments during the journey surprised you, moments of insight, connection, or inner stillness that you did not expect?**

Think about the days that felt like turning points. What happened, and how did they move you?

4. **As you look ahead, how will you carry this heart-centred way of living into your daily life, and what intentions will guide the next chapter of your journey?** Nathan discovered that this was more than a program, it was a way of being. What will your heart ask of you now?

Each of these questions is designed to help you, like Nathan, integrate the transformation you have experienced and move forward with intention, awareness, and an unbound heart.

**Affirmations For You – (Heart Whispers)**

Affirmations have the power to quiet the noise of doubt, open the doorway to self-trust, and draw you back into the wisdom of your heart. When practised daily, they nurture an inner dialogue based in love and truth, helping you live each day more aligned with who you truly are. I invite you to repeat silently or write:

- *I listen to my heart's whispers and follow its guidance.*
- *I embrace vulnerability and allow my heart to lead the way.*
- *I nurture my self–compassion and connect with my heart.*
- *I choose to align with my heart's deepest desires and values.*
- *I practice gratitude to open my heart to the abundance of life.*
- *I trust the wisdom of my heart to guide me towards a fulfilling and authentic life.*

**Integration Circle & Future Intentions**

This practice is designed to help you anchor the wisdom of your journey and carry it into your daily life with clarity and intention. Integration is where transformation takes root, not just in your mind, but in your heart, relationships, and choices. Whether you are in a group or reflecting individually, take your time with this process:

1. **Identify Three Key Learnings**: Pause and consider the most powerful lessons you have received during this program. These may be insights about yourself, truths about how you connect with others, or practices that have shifted your perspective. Write them down clearly and concisely, as if you are creating guideposts to return to.

2. **Share Two Emotional Shifts**: Reflect on the inner changes you have felt along the way. Perhaps you moved from fear to trust, from tension to calm, from loneliness to connection, or from self-criticism to self-compassion. Sharing these shifts, with yourself in writing, or with others if in a circle, helps you honour your growth and embody the change.
3. **Set One Heartfelt Intention Moving Forward**: Ask your heart: *"What do I want to carry into my next chapter?"* This intention may be simple yet profound, such as *"I choose presence," "I honour my heart daily,"* or *"I live with openness and courage."* Anchor it in words that feel alive and real for you.
4. **Record and Revisit**: Write your reflections on a *"Heart Integration Commitment"* card or in your journal. Place this somewhere you will see it often, a reminder on your desk, a note in your wallet, or a page you return to weekly. As you revisit your reflections, allow them to evolve, deepening your sense of alignment and accountability.

**Optional Closing Ritual**: To seal the circle or personal reflection, place your hand over your heart, take three slow breaths, and silently repeat: *"I carry my learnings. I honour my shifts. I walk with intention."*

**Closing Reflection**

You have walked a sacred path, through breath, gratitude, stillness, courage, creativity, vulnerability, and now, reflection. This is not the end of your journey. It is a quiet threshold. A moment to pause, gather what you have learned, and honour the growth that has unfolded within you. Reflection invites you to hold your story with gentleness. To see not only what happened, but *how you have changed.* It is in this space that healing becomes wisdom, and experience becomes purpose. You are not who you were when you began. You carry more insight, more softness, more strength. Through reflection, you begin to integrate all the lessons, all the emotions, all the heartbeats of this journey, and you begin to see yourself more clearly. So take this moment to honour yourself. Not for being perfect, but for showing up. For feeling deeply. For choosing truth. For choosing your heart. As you step into whatever comes next, carry this with you: *Your story matters. Your heart knows the way, and every pause to reflect is a powerful step forward.* Let this final part not be a closing, but a deepening. Let reflection be the thread that ties your inner work to your outer world, and let your unbound heart continue to lead you, home to yourself, again and again.

**The Invitation Continues**

You have begun something meaningful. Every Unbound offering, book or program, is an invitation to go deeper. If something in you whispered "yes" while reading this module, honour it. Continue the journey – www.timetotransform.world

# MODULE 12 – HOMECOMING

**Your Opening Reflection**

**Invitation to Return to Your Heart -** As you step into this module, I invite you to come with gentleness, as though you are walking through the door of your own inner sanctuary. Homecoming is not about arriving somewhere new, but about remembering what has always been within you. Let this be a space where you release the weight of masks, roles, and striving, and allow yourself to rest in the truth of who you are. Here, you are safe. Here, you are whole. Here, you are home.

- "When in your life have you felt most at home within yourself? What did it feel like in your body, heart, and spirit?"
- "Where have you been searching outside of yourself for belonging or approval? How has that search shaped your journey?"
- "What truths about yourself have you reclaimed through this program that remind you of your wholeness?"
- "What masks, roles, or stories are you now ready to lay down so that you can return more fully to your authentic self?"
- "If your heart could speak to you right now as you arrive "home," what would it want you to hear and carry forward?"

Let these questions open the doorway into presence. Every answer you give, whether in words, sensations, or silence, is a bridge between where you are and where you are going.

## Learning Objectives

The learning objectives are included here to give you a clear focus for this module, ensuring that each practice you explore moves you closer to mastering the skills, insights, and heart-led awareness that will enrich your life well beyond the program. By the end of this module, you will:

- Reframe your journey as a return to your authentic self, rather than an escape from your past.
- Recognise your heart as your true home, a place of safety, acceptance, and belonging.
- Celebrate wholeness and authenticity by embracing the truth that you are already enough.
- Apply daily practices of homecoming (breath, silence, reflection, gratitude) to ground yourself in presence.
- Experience the freedom of belonging by releasing the need for external validation and trusting your inner sanctuary.
- Integrate your entire *Unbound* journey into your daily life, carrying forward its wisdom with clarity and courage.

## Core Emotional Domains

The core emotional intelligence domains covered here are essential because they form the foundation for lasting heart connection, guiding you to deepen self-awareness, regulate emotions, build resilience, and strengthen the mind-body bond throughout your *Unbound* journey.

- **Self-Awareness:** Recognising inner truth and wholeness. Cultivating awareness of when you feel most *"at home"* within yourself.
- **Self-Regulation:** Developing daily grounding practices to stay centred. Returning to presence when distracted or unsettled.
- **Motivation (Heart-Aligned Purpose);** Living from authenticity rather than external approval. Strengthening inner commitment to values and truth.
- **Empathy:** Honouring your own journey while respecting others' paths of return. Creating space for deeper human connection through belonging.

- **Social Skills (Authentic Connection);** Engaging with others from a place of self-acceptance. Building trust and connection by embodying wholeness and presence.

## "Homecoming – Returning To The Deepest Truth Of Who You Are"

Homecoming is not about reaching a final destination, but about recognising that the journey has always been leading you inward, toward the centre of your being. After walking through the valleys of self-doubt, climbing the mountains of growth, and crossing the rivers of release, you arrive not at a place outside of yourself, but at the quiet sanctuary that has always lived within your heart. This is the sacred return to the deepest truth of who you are. It is the realisation that you were never lost, only learning. You were never broken, only becoming. You were never incomplete, only waiting to remember your wholeness. Homecoming is the gentle unveiling of your authentic self, the part of you untouched by fear, beyond masks, beyond roles, beyond the expectations of others. To come home is to lay down the armour you no longer need. It is to embrace yourself without conditions, to rest in your own presence with love and acceptance. It is to finally recognise that freedom was never about escape, but about alignment, the alignment of your life with the wisdom of your heart. Here, you no longer strive to be someone else, because you remember that you already are enough. You already belong. You already carry the sanctuary you seek.

This module is a celebration of integration. It gathers together all the pieces of your journey, the lessons, the tears, the laughter, the breakthroughs, the silences, and weaves them into a tapestry of belonging. Homecoming honours not just what you have discovered, but who you have become in the process. It invites you to pause, to look back with gratitude, and to see how far you have come, not with pride alone, but with reverence for the courage it took to arrive here, and so, the invitation now is not simply to reflect, but to embody. To live your homecoming daily, in the way you speak, in the choices you make, in how you hold yourself and others. To anchor yourself in the present moment, to keep returning to your heart, again and again, until the rhythm of authenticity becomes your natural way of being. Homecoming is both a resting and a beginning. It is the quiet whisper that says: *"Welcome home. You are whole. You are free. You belong."*

### The Journey As A Return

For much of your life, you may have believed that transformation meant reaching for something outside yourself, a new role to play, a new identity to claim, or a new horizon to chase. Perhaps you thought healing meant becoming someone different, stronger, braver, or more worthy than you once believed yourself to be, but as you stand here now, you can see more clearly: the true journey was never about escaping, fixing, or becoming. It was about remembering, uncovering, and returning. Every step you have taken, whether steady or stumbling, whether lit by joy or shrouded in pain, has been leading you back to a truth that was always yours: *you are already whole.* The wounds you carried, the doubts you wrestled with, the ways you once hid yourself were not proof of something missing in you. They were invitations, signals pointing you inward, urging you to peel back the layers of fear, conditioning, and expectation so that your heart could be revealed. Wholeness was never broken. It was simply veiled. Beneath the noise of external demands and the pressure to become someone else, your essence remained intact, quietly waiting for your return, and through courage, vulnerability, and a willingness to look honestly at yourself, you have begun to uncover it again. To understand the journey as a return is to release the belief that home lies in some faraway place or future version of you. Instead, it reminds you that home has always been here, in your breath, in your body, and in the quiet wisdom of your heart. Every experience, even the ones you thought were detours or failures, has been part of the path leading you home.

When you embrace this truth, you stop searching for completion in external validation, success, or approval. You no longer need to outrun your past, because you see it now not as a weight that held you back, but as a teacher that walked beside you. Every challenge, every moment of breaking, every breakthrough was not about losing yourself, but about finding your way back. Coming home is not about arrival in the sense of finality. It is about awakening to the reality that you already carry everything you were seeking. The love, the safety, the belonging, the freedom, all of it has always been part of you. You need only pause, breathe, and listen to remember. So today, let this truth settle into your heart: *You have not been wandering aimlessly. You have been on the most sacred pilgrimage of all the journey of returning to yourself.*

## Your Heart As Home

There is a place within you that has never abandoned you, even in the moments when you felt furthest from yourself. This place is steady, unshaken, and whole. It is not dependent on external approval, success, or circumstance. It does not ask you to perform, prove, or perfect. It simply waits, with quiet patience, for you to remember it. This place is your heart, your truest home. Your heart does not keep score of how far you have wandered, how long you stayed away, or how many times you doubted your worth. Like a faithful sanctuary, it remains open, steady, and ready to welcome you back. No matter what paths you have taken, through struggle, through self-doubt, through distraction or detour, the heart always holds the doorway to belonging. You cannot lose it, because you are it. To recognise your heart as home is to understand that you already carry within you the safety, the peace, and the belonging you have longed for. It is to realise that the love you have sought in others, the security you have craved from the world, and the permission you have waited for to be yourself have always been present inside of you. Your heart has been whispering all along: *You belong here. You belong to yourself.* When you begin to trust your heart in this way, you stop chasing validation in external sources. You stop bending yourself into shapes to be accepted or loved. You stop looking for home in people, places, or outcomes that can never provide lasting safety. Instead, you rest in the truth that you belong first to yourself, that your value is not contingent upon anyone else seeing it, but on your own willingness to honour it. Coming home to your heart is not about building walls to keep others out; it is about creating roots so that you can meet the world with openness and authenticity. From this grounded centre, you can give and receive love without fear of losing yourself. You can walk through uncertainty with courage, because your anchor is no longer outside of you. This is the sacred shift: to live not from the fragile house of external approval, but from the eternal sanctuary of your heart. Here, you find freedom. Here, you find peace. Here, you know beyond doubt: *I am safe. I am whole. I am already home.*

**Heart-Anchor Practice: Coming Home to Yourself**

1. **Find Your Space**: Sit somewhere quiet where you can be undisturbed. Place both feet on the ground and let your body soften into the chair or cushion beneath you. Allow your shoulders to drop.
2. **Place Your Hand Over Your Heart**: Gently place one or both hands on your heart space. Feel the warmth of your palms. Notice the rise and fall of your chest as you breathe.
3. **Breathe Into Home**: Take three slow, steady breaths, imagining that each inhale fills your heart with light and each exhale clears away any

heaviness, doubt, or distraction. With each breath, whisper inwardly: *I am home.*

4. **Listen to the Whisper Within**: Ask your heart: *What do you want me to know right now?* Do not rush or force an answer. Simply listen. It may come as a word, an image, a feeling, or a sense of stillness. Trust whatever arises.
5. **Anchor the Belonging**: Say to yourself silently or aloud: *"I belong to myself. My heart is my sanctuary. I am always welcome here."*
6. **Carry It Forward**: Before you leave the practice, choose one small way to honour your heart today, perhaps speaking kindly to yourself, pausing to breathe before a decision, or giving yourself rest.

You can adapt this into a **short ritual** at the start or end of each day. The more often you return to it, the more natural it becomes to feel at home within yourself, wherever you are.

**Wholeness And Authenticity**

Wholeness is the quiet yet radical act of recognising that nothing about you is missing. For years, you may have carried the belief that you had to earn your worth, achieve more, heal everything, or somehow *"fix"* yourself in order to be complete, but the truth is simpler and more profound: you were always whole. What looked like brokenness was often only a part of you waiting to be seen with love. What felt like lack was often a story learned from others, not the truth of your being. To live in wholeness does not mean you will never feel pain, doubt, or fear. It means that when those moments arise, you do not exile them. Instead, you welcome them as part of your human experience, knowing they do not define you, but simply move through you. You begin to see that the cracks in your story are not flaws to hide but openings where light enters. You understand that your tenderness is strength, your vulnerability is wisdom, and your imperfections are what make your humanity beautiful. Authenticity emerges naturally from this state of wholeness. When you stop abandoning yourself in search of approval or safety, you find the courage to show up as you truly are. Authenticity is not about being loud or dramatic; it is about being real. It is in the moments you say what you mean, honour your boundaries, or allow yourself to be seen without pretence. It is in choosing to live from the inside out, rather than from the outside in. Living from the truth of *"I am enough"* becomes a daily practice of alignment. Some days it may feel like a whisper, soft, uncertain, yet steady. Other days it may roar through you with conviction. Either way, it is a truth that does not depend on perfection, performance, or permission. It is a declaration that your worth is intrinsic, that your presence matters, and that you belong exactly as you are. This wholeness and authenticity ripple outward. As you live more honestly with yourself, your relationships begin to shift. You stop performing roles that keep you safe but small. You stop hiding your light for fear of rejection. Instead, you allow others to meet the real you, raw, kind, flawed, radiant. Some connections may fall away, but those that remain will be deeper, truer, and more life-giving. To embody this wholeness is to rest in the deepest kind of freedom: the freedom of being at home in your own skin. It is to wake each morning and remember that you do not have to earn the right to exist, to love, or to shine. You already are enough. You always were.

### Daily Practices Of Homecoming

To live a life of homecoming is to recognise that wholeness is not found in faraway places but in the rhythm of your everyday presence. It is in the breath you take before speaking, in the stillness you create when you pause, in the gratitude you whisper before sleep. These are not small acts; they are doorways. Each ritual, however ordinary it may seem, is a portal through which you return to your heart, your true home.

**Breath** becomes your anchor. With each inhale, you invite life into your body; with each exhale, you release what no longer serves you. Slowly, breath reminds you that you are safe to be here, now. The world outside may be noisy or uncertain, but one conscious breath restores clarity. In this way, breath is not simply oxygen, it is a sacred thread that ties you back to yourself.

**Silence** is your sanctuary. In a world filled with constant demands and noise, choosing even a few moments of quiet is a radical act of love. In silence, the heart whispers what the mind forgets. It tells you that you are enough, that you are held, that you are already whole. Silence invites you to stop performing and simply be. Within this stillness, the ground of your being steadies.

**Reflection** is the mirror of your soul. It allows you to see the patterns of your journey with honesty and compassion. Reflection transforms your experiences into wisdom, helping you understand not only what has happened but also how it has shaped you. When you pause to reflect, you gather the fragments of your life and weave them into a story of resilience, growth, and grace.

**Gratitude** is the lens that reveals the sacred in the ordinary. When you give thanks for a sunrise, a smile, or even your own breath, you turn simple moments into holy ground. Gratitude softens your heart and makes space for joy. It reminds you that abundance is not something you wait for, it is something you awaken to by noticing what is already here, but perhaps the deepest truth of daily homecoming is this: **it is not about perfection, but return.** You will forget. You will get caught up in distraction, worry, or self-judgment. Yet every time you pause, to breathe, to be still, to reflect, to give thanks, you come home again. That return, however gentle, is the essence of love.

Over time, these rituals cease to feel like practices you must remember. They become the natural rhythm of your life. The breath becomes a prayer. Silence becomes your resting place. Reflection becomes wisdom embodied. Gratitude becomes the language of your heart. Through daily homecoming, you learn that love is not only an offering you give outward but also a devotion you extend inward. This is how you root yourself in presence, not as a fleeting moment but as a way of being. When you return again and again to your heart, you discover the truth that has been waiting all along: you were never truly lost. Your home has always been here.

## The Freedom Of Belonging

Belonging is one of the deepest human longings, yet for much of life, we are conditioned to search for it outside ourselves. We seek it in relationships, workplaces, communities, achievements, and approval. We mould ourselves to fit expectations, edit our truth to gain acceptance, and sometimes abandon pieces of who we are just to feel included, and yet, no matter how much we achieve, how many circles we fit into, or how much praise we receive, there can remain a quiet emptiness, a sense that we are still not *enough*. The heart knows differently. True belonging does not begin outside of you, it begins within you. The freedom of belonging is the moment you finally recognise that you do not have to earn your place here. You already belong, simply because you exist. This is not arrogance, but alignment with truth: the universe, life itself, has already said yes to you. Your very breath is evidence that you are meant to be here. When you remember this, you are freed from the constant weight of external validation. You no longer need to contort yourself into someone else's idea of worthy. You no longer hand over the keys of your identity to others. Instead, you reclaim the sanctuary of your own heart. This is the freedom of belonging: the relief of resting in yourself, without condition, and with this freedom comes courage, because when you know you belong to yourself, you no longer fear rejection in the same way. You can step forward authentically, even when it feels risky, because your worth is no longer up for debate. You can walk into the world with balance, because you are no longer pulled apart by the competing expectations of others. You are free to be steady, centred, and true, even in the midst of chaos.

Paradoxically, when you no longer seek belonging outside yourself, your connections with others actually deepen. Instead of approaching relationships from need, performance, or fear, you meet others with openness. You are able to love without clinging, to listen without defensiveness, and to share without pretense. Your authenticity becomes an invitation, allowing others to feel safe in their own. This is the great paradox of belonging: when you stop chasing it, you begin to experience it everywhere. The freedom of belonging is also the freedom to live fully. To laugh without worrying how you look. To create without fearing failure. To love without shrinking back. It is the courage to move through the world as your whole self, not perfect, but present, not flawless, but free, and so, Homecoming leads you here: to the truth that your heart has been whispering all along. *You are already home. You are already whole. You are already enough.* When you carry this knowing, belonging is no longer something to seek, it is something you embody.

**Walking Home to Your Heart Exercise**

**Step 1: Create a Sacred Space:** Find a quiet place where you can be undisturbed for at least 20 minutes. Dim the lights, light a candle if you wish, and place your hand gently over your heart. Breathe slowly, as if you are arriving somewhere safe.

**Step 2: Visualisation – The Path Home:** Close your eyes and imagine yourself standing on a path that leads back to your true home. This is not a physical house, but an inner sanctuary where your heart waits for you. Begin walking this path in your mind's eye:

- Notice what it looks like. Is it forested, sandy, lit by lanterns, or open sky?
- Feel each step releasing old stories, masks, or burdens you no longer need to carry.
- As you walk, repeat silently: *I am coming home.*

When you reach the doorway of your sanctuary, pause. Place your hand on the door. Feel its warmth, its invitation. When you are ready, step inside.

**Step 3: Enter the Sanctuary:** Inside, you find a space that reflects your truest self. Notice the colours, the sounds, the stillness. In the centre of the room is a mirror, but unlike any you have ever seen. As you look into it, you do not see flaws, mistakes, or masks, you see your whole, radiant, authentic self. Greet this self with love. Whisper: *Welcome home.*

**Step 4: Heart Declaration:** Now, take a journal and write a **Homecoming Declaration** to yourself. Begin with:

- *I am home when…* (list the moments you feel most grounded and true)
- *I am whole because…* (honour the strengths, lessons, and truths you have reclaimed)
- *I choose to honour my homecoming by…* (name one daily act that will keep you connected in your heart).

**Step 5: Embody the Ritual:** Close by placing both hands over your heart and saying three times, slowly and with presence: ***"I am home. I am whole. I am free."*** Sit in silence for a few moments. Allow the words to settle in your body like roots anchoring you deeply into the ground of your being.

**Why this matters:** This exercise moves readers from *concept* into *embodiment.* It helps them not only understand Homecoming but **feel it, see it**, and **anchor it into a daily practice** that continues beyond the program.

**Dr John McSwiney's Journey Back To His Heartspace**

There was a long season in my life when the rhythm of busyness drowned out the rhythm of my heart. On the outside, it looked as though I had everything together: career achievements, responsibilities fulfilled, the appearance of stability. Yet on the inside, I was running on empty. My heart whispered for stillness, for authenticity, for peace, for love, but I silenced it with more work, more striving, more proving. The turning point did not arrive as a dramatic event, but as a quiet, persistent ache. A deep knowing that would no longer let me ignore it. I remember one morning by the ocean, standing barefoot in the sand as the waves moved with their timeless rhythm. I placed my hand on my chest and realised, with a shock of sadness, that I could no longer feel myself. I had been so focused on being who I thought the world wanted me to be that I had forgotten the deeper truth of who I already was. That realisation did not break me with fear, but stirred me with longing, a longing to come home to my heart, to lay down the mask, to return to the one I was always created to be. The journey back was not quick. It was tender, awkward, and often uncomfortable. I began in small ways: three conscious breaths before stepping into the day, a few unedited lines in a journal, moments of allowing my heart to speak without judgement. I gave myself permission to feel, to truly feel, the grief I had buried, the joy I had muted, and the love I had postponed. Slowly, almost imperceptibly, my heart began to respond.

There were glimmers of clarity and peace that arose not from doing, but simply from being. The ocean became my teacher again. Out on the waves, saltwater and sun on my skin, I remembered the boy who once surfed with wonder, laughed without hesitation, and lived unmasked. He was still there, waiting patiently for me to invite him home. Reconnecting with my heartspace revealed a profound truth: wholeness was not something I needed to chase or achieve. It was not found in accolades, approval, or perfection. It was found in the quiet courage to meet myself with honesty, grace and compassion. It was found when I chose to listen to my heart, even when it trembled, even when it felt uncomfortable and inconvenient. My life today is not flawless, but it is aligned. I live from my heartspace not because it is easy, but because it is the only way I know how to live fully, authentically, and free. This journey of homecoming is ongoing. Every breath, every choice, every act of love is another step toward my heart, another step home.

**Reflection Exercise: Dr John's Journey**

1. **Where in your own life has busyness, proving, or striving drowned out the quiet rhythm of your heart?** Take a moment to

notice if there are areas where you look accomplished on the outside but feel empty or disconnected within.

2. **What 'mask' or role have you worn to meet others' expectations, and what truth lies beneath it, waiting to be remembered?** Reflect on the parts of yourself that long to be seen without performance or pretence.
3. **What small, gentle practices could you begin today, like breath, journaling, or silence, to reconnect with your inner sanctuary?** Consider not the grand gestures, but the tender beginnings that open space for your heart to speak again.
4. **If you were to return to the *"you"* who once lived with wonder, joy, and freedom, what would you reclaim, and how would that change the way you show up in your life now?** Let your imagination guide you back to the essence of who you were before striving overshadowed your being.

**Affirmations For You – (Heart Whispers)**

Affirmations have the power to quiet the noise of doubt, open the doorway to self-trust, and draw you back into the wisdom of your heart. When practised daily, they nurture an inner dialogue based in love and truth, helping you live each day more aligned with who you truly are. I invite you to repeat silently or write:

- *I already am enough; nothing is missing.*
- *I return again and again to the deepest truth of who I am.*
- *Wholeness is not something I chase, it is who I already am.*
- *I release the masks and walk in the freedom of authenticity.*
- *Every breath brings me back home to my heart.*
- *I honour my journey, my struggles, and my becoming with compassion.*
- *I walk forward in courage, grace, and love, because I am already home.*

**Guided Journaling Exercise: Returning Home to Your Heart**

**Step 1 – Pause and Arrive**: Take three slow, conscious breaths. Place your hand gently over your heart. Whisper softly: *"I am here. I am listening."*

**Step 2 – Reflection Prompts**: Write freely and without editing. Let your heart guide your pen.

- Where in your life has busyness or striving drowned out the rhythm of your heart? Describe the places where you appear successful on the outside but feel empty within.
- What mask or role have you worn to meet others' expectations? Who or what have you been trying to prove yourself to? What truth lies beneath that mask, waiting to be remembered?
- What small daily practices could reconnect you with your inner sanctuary? Breath, journaling, silence, or something else? Write down one practice you will commit to this week.
- If you returned to the *"you"* who lived with wonder, joy, and freedom, what would you reclaim? Recall the child, the younger self, or the part of you who laughed freely and lived unmasked. Describe them. What gift does that part of you want to give you now?

**Step 3 – Integration** Re-read what you have written. Circle or underline the words or phrases that feel most alive to you. These are your heart's signals.

**Step 4 – Closing Ritual** Place your hand on your heart again. Say aloud three times: *"I am coming home. I am enough. I am free."* Then sit in silence for a few moments. Notice what rises in you, peace, tears, longing, gratitude, and simply allow it to be.

**Closing Reflection**

Coming home is not a destination you reach, it is the quiet remembrance of what has always been within you. It is the soft return to the truth that you are not broken, not lacking, not lost. You are, and have always been, whole. The journey of *Unbound* has carried you through breath and silence, gratitude and affirmation, laughter and tears, reflection and release. Each step has not taken you somewhere else, but has led you closer to yourself. Homecoming is the moment you realise that all along, the sanctuary you were seeking was already beating in your chest. To come home is to no longer abandon yourself in the pursuit of approval. It is to no longer silence your heart for fear of rejection. It is to choose presence over performance, compassion over perfection, love over fear. Homecoming is the sacred act of standing in your own light and saying: *"I belong here. I belong to me."* Let this be your reminder: You do not have to keep searching for what you already carry. You are the hearth. You are the sanctuary. You are the home, and every time you pause, every time you breathe, every time you listen, you return again. So as you close this module, carry this truth with you: the journey of transformation is not about becoming someone new. It is about remembering who you have always been. When you live from this place, every moment becomes a homecoming. Every choice, an act of love. Every breath, a step closer to freedom.

**Transformation Loves Momentum**

Do not stop now. Momentum is a sacred energy, once it moves, let it carry you. Another Unbound chapter, book, or online experience will help you keep that energy alive – www.timetotransform.world

# WHAT COMES NEXT - LIVING AND PRACTISING UNBOUND

This book concludes, but nothing here is finished. If it has done its work, you will not be closing these pages with a sense of completion, but with a heightened awareness, of yourself, of your practice, and of the quiet choices that shape both. What you carry forward is not a method to be applied wholesale, but a way of seeing more clearly how you practise law, and how the law practises you in return. The question at this point is not *what to do next*. It is *how to continue*.

## FROM READING TO PRACTICE

Lawyers are trained to extract principles and apply them. This book resists that impulse, deliberately. What you have encountered here is not a set of techniques to be deployed when convenient, but a recalibration of the internal conditions that govern judgment, conduct, and endurance. The real work begins not in reflection, but in the return to ordinary professional moments: the email written under pressure, the conversation held when patience is thin, the decision made when certainty is unavailable. Living unbound does not announce itself. It is rarely visible to others. It shows up quietly:

- in the pause you take before responding
- in the tone you choose when authority would allow sharpness
- in the boundary you hold without justification
- in the decision to rest rather than push beyond clarity

These are not small acts. They are the cumulative architecture of a professional life lived with integrity. Transformation in law is not dramatic.

It is disciplined.

## INTEGRATING THIS WORK INTO YOUR LEGAL LIFE

There is no expectation that this book will be absorbed evenly or practised uniformly. Some lawyers will return repeatedly to the foundations, breath, grounding, reflection, because the intensity of their work demands continual stabilisation. Others will work more consciously with language, listening, and focus, refining how they influence and lead within complex environments. Many will find that the deepest work unfolds later, when forgiveness, kindness, and homecoming become essential responses to long-carried weight. This is not a linear journey. It is cyclical. You may move fluidly between sections depending on the season of your practice. Periods of high intensity may call for steadiness. Periods of disillusionment may call for purpose. Periods of authority may call for restraint. The work adapts because the profession does. What matters is not how often you return to these practices, but that you recognise when return is required.

## PRACTISING UNBOUND WITHIN SYSTEMS OF POWER

Living unbound does not remove you from the structures of law. It does not exempt you from hierarchy, duty, or constraint. It changes how you inhabit them. Law is exercised within systems, courts, firms, agencies, institutions, that carry their own pressures, incentives, and imperfections. Practising unbound does not deny this reality. It acknowledges it honestly and asks a more demanding question: *How will you remain ethically coherent within it?*. Unbound practice allows you to:

- hold authority without identifying with it
- work within imperfect systems without becoming cynical
- exercise power without diminishing others
- meet institutional pressure without abandoning personal standards

This is not idealism. It is professional maturity. To practise unbound is to accept that you cannot control every outcome, but you can remain accountable for how you participate in producing them.

## CARRYING THIS WORK FORWARD

Some lawyers will carry this work privately, allowing it to quietly recalibrate their internal compass. Others will recognise its relevance to leadership, teaching, supervision, or cultural change within their organisations. Neither path is superior. This book does not ask you to persuade others, introduce new language, or declare a philosophy. It asks you to practise differently, and to let that difference be felt through conduct rather than explanation. In law, example carries more weight than argument. Over time, clarity becomes visible. Presence becomes reliable. Boundaries become respected. Influence deepens without force. This is how change most often occurs in the profession, not through reform alone, but through individuals who practise with steadiness others can trust.

## THE LONG VIEW - LAW AS A LIFE, NOT A SEASON

Many legal careers falter not because lawyers fail, but because they succeed for too long without integration. They endure. They achieve. They adapt. And gradually, the work narrows rather than deepens them. This book was written to interrupt that trajectory. A life in law is not meant to be survived. It is meant to be lived with coherence, where skill is matched by judgment, ambition by conscience, and endurance by meaning. Your legacy will not be shaped only by cases won, positions held, or reputations earned. It will be shaped by:

- how you treated people when the stakes were high
- how you used authority when restraint was possible
- how you responded when outcomes disappointed
- how you remained human when the work encouraged distance

These are the measures that endure.

## A FINAL WORD

If you take nothing else from this book, take this: You do not need to become a different kind of lawyer. You need only to practise as a more integrated one. Strong without hardness. Clear without cruelty. Committed without self-erasure. The law does not require you to abandon your humanity in order to serve it well. On the contrary, it depends on your humanity to remain worthy of service. This is what it means to live and practise unbound. Not apart from the profession. Not above it, but fully, responsibly, and consciously within it, across a lifetime in the law.

Time To Transform

EMPOWERING LIVES

# YOU ARE NOT ALONE

Legal practice carries weight. The responsibility to advise, decide, advocate, and hold consequence over time can be deeply meaningful, and, at times, profoundly demanding. As you move through *The Unbound Lawyer*, you may encounter moments where reflection brings to the surface strain that has been quietly carried, often without language or acknowledgement. This is not failure. It is the human cost of professional responsibility. Lawyers are trained to manage pressure, to remain composed, and to be the steady presence others rely upon. Over time, this can make it difficult to recognise when support is needed, or to ask for it. Yet the ability to seek help when required is not a weakness. It is a professional act of judgment and care. Support matters particularly when:

- the cumulative burden of work feels heavy or unrelenting
- stress, fatigue, or emotional strain begin to interfere with clarity or wellbeing
- you are carrying responsibility in isolation
- you need to speak openly, without expectation, explanation, or agenda

Reaching out is not an abdication of strength. It is an exercise of it. It protects the person who practises the law, and, by extension, the quality of judgment the profession depends upon. The services listed below are confidential, free, and available to you at any time.

## SUPPORT SERVICES

### Australia

- **Lifeline Australia** - 13 11 14 (24/7 crisis support and suicide prevention)

- **Beyond Blue** - 1300 22 4636 (24/7 support for anxiety, depression, and mental health concerns)
- **Kids Helpline** - 1800 55 1800 (24/7 support for young people aged 5–25)
- **Suicide Call Back Service** - 1300 659 467 (24/7 counselling for people at risk and their carers)

**New Zealand**

- **Lifeline New Zealand** - 0800 543 354 or text 4357 (24/7 support)
- **1737 – Need to Talk?** - Call or text 1737 (24/7 access to trained counsellors)
- **Youthline** - 0800 376 633 or text 234 (Support for young people)

**United States**

- **988 Suicide & Crisis Lifeline** - Call or text 988 (24/7 support for anyone in crisis)
- **NAMI Helpline** 1-800-950-NAMI (Mon–Fri, 10am–10pm ET)
- **Crisis Text Line** Text **HOME** to 741741 (24/7 text-based support)

**Canada**

- **Talk Suicide Canada** - 1-833-456-4566 or text 45645 (24/7 support)
- **Kids Help Phone** - 1-800-668-6868 or text **CONNECT** to 686868 (24/7 support for young people)
- **Wellness Together Canada** - 1-866-585-0445 (24/7 mental health and substance use support)

**United Kingdom**

- **Samaritans** - 116 123 (24/7 support for emotional distress)
- **Mind Infoline** - 0300 123 3393 (Mental health support and information)
- **Shout Crisis Text Line** - Text **SHOUT** to 85258 (24/7 text support)

## A FINAL WORD ON SUPPORT

Seeking support is not a retreat from responsibility. It is a way of sustaining it. The law depends on practitioners who are clear, grounded, and capable of judgment under pressure. Attending to your own wellbeing is part of maintaining that capacity. When you reach out, whether by calling, texting, or speaking with someone trained to listen, you are exercising care for yourself and for the work you carry. This journey was never meant to be undertaken alone. Just as you are learning to practise with greater awareness and restraint, these services exist to offer support when the weight feels too heavy to carry on your own. They are there to listen, without judgment, and without expectation. Keep this page close. Support is always within reach.

# YOUR UNBOUND JOURNEY SERIES

Completing *The Unbound Lawyer* marks the beginning of a broader journey within the **Unbound Series**. Each book in the series has a distinct purpose, audience, and depth, while remaining grounded in the same heart-centred philosophy. You are encouraged to choose your next step based on **where you are now**, rather than where you think you should be.

## THE UNBOUND SERIES – CORE BOOKS

**Heart Unbound: The Ultimate 28 Day Heart Connection Challenge** - The gentle, guided, and grounded introduction to the Unbound Series. This book establishes the foundations of presence, self-awareness, emotional regulation, compassion, and integration. It is designed as an accessible entry point for individuals beginning their Unbound journey.

**Time to Transform: Living Unbound** - The flagship *magnus opus* work of *Time to Transform*. This book forms the philosophical, practical, and conceptual foundation from which all Unbound Series books are drawn. It is a comprehensive handbook for life transformation, integrating heart-centred awareness into everyday living.

**The Unbound Leader** - Designed for leaders at all levels, this book explores heart-led leadership, emotional intelligence, ethical decision-making, and sustainable performance. It supports leaders seeking to align personal integrity with professional responsibility.

**The Unbound Organisation** - Focused on building cultures of connection, courage, and compassion, this book supports organisations navigating wellbeing, leadership development, and cultural renewal. It translates Unbound principles into organisational and systemic contexts.

**The Unbound Student** - Tailored for students and emerging leaders, this book supports self-awareness, resilience, identity formation, and purposeful learning. It provides a grounded framework for personal growth during formative educational and life stages.

**Time to Transform: Evidence Companion** - Provides the research, theory, and professional assurance that underpin the heart-centred practices of the Unbound Series.

## CHOOSING YOUR NEXT STEP

There is no required order in which to read the Unbound Series. Each book stands alone while contributing to a unified body of work. You may choose to continue with deeper personal exploration, leadership development, organisational application, or long-term integration. What matters is **alignment, not progression**.

## CONTINUING WITH TIME TO TRANSFORM

The Unbound Series is part of the broader *Time to Transform* ecosystem, which includes programs, facilitated experiences, and sector-specific applications across leadership, education, wellbeing, and organisational development. To explore the full range of books and programs, visit: www.timetotransform.world

***Your journey does not end here. It continues with clarity, structure, and heart.***

# CONTINUE YOUR UNBOUND JOURNEY

Every Unbound book is part of a wider ecosystem of transformation:

- Online Courses
- Leadership Programs
- Heart-Connection Challenges
- Student Success Pathways
- Organisational Wellbeing Systems
- Celtic-Inspired Emotional Intelligence Journeys
- Live Events & Workshops
- Author Community & Resources

You are invited to take the next step - deeper, braver, wiser.

**All paths begin here:**

www.timetotransform.world

**THE UNBOUND CALL**

*There is always a deeper breath to take, a truer story to live, and a wider life waiting for you. When you are ready to walk further, the Unbound Path will meet you there.*

The Unbound Series

Closing Note

# CLOSING NOTE

Pause here before you move on. Take a moment to consider:

- how you currently carry the weight of your work
- where you have become hardened, and where you have remained open
- what kind of lawyer you are becoming through daily practice

There is no judgment in these questions. Only invitation. The law will continue to demand precision, courage, and endurance. It will place you in moments of conflict, uncertainty, and consequence. It will test not only what you know, but who you are when knowing is not enough. When those moments arise, remember this:

- You are allowed to pause.
- You are allowed to reflect.
- You are allowed to practise with conscience as well as competence.

Justice does not ask for your self-erasure. It asks for your presence. May you practise with clarity when pressure rises. May you speak with restraint when power is yours. May you remain kind without becoming naive, and strong without becoming hard, and may the law, through you, remain worthy of the trust placed in it.

# CONTINUING PROFESSIONAL DEVELOPMENT (CPD) - PROFESSIONAL USE STATEMENT

*The Unbound Lawyer* is designed to support ongoing professional development, ethical practice, and psychosocial sustainability across a legal career. This book may be used by practising lawyers as a **self-directed CPD activity**, where permitted under applicable CPD rules, particularly in the areas of:

- **Ethics and Professional Responsibility**
- **Professional Skills**
- **Practice Management and Business Skills**
- **Wellbeing, Resilience, and Fitness to Practise**

The framework and practices contained in this book focus on reflective judgment, ethical decision-making, communication, focus, emotional regulation, and responsible use of authority, all of which are recognised components of competent legal practice.

## Suggested CPD Hours (Guide Only)

Lawyers may claim CPD hours commensurate with:

- time spent reading and reflecting on the material
- completion of reflective exercises or journalling
- application of practices to live legal matters
- participation in peer discussion, supervision, or facilitated sessions

As a general guide:

- **Reading and reflective engagement**: 1–4 CPD hours
- **Structured reflection and application**: 2–6 CPD hours
- **Facilitated or group-based engagement**: hours as delivered

Lawyers should retain their own records and self-assess compliance with local CPD requirements.

## 2. FORMAL CPD LEARNING OUTCOMES (AUDIT-READY)

### Learning Outcomes

On completion of *The Unbound Lawyer* (and associated reflective activities), participants will be able to:

- apply reflective practice to ethical and professional dilemmas in legal contexts
- exercise clearer judgment and restraint under pressure
- communicate with greater precision, presence, and professionalism
- regulate emotional response in high-stakes or adversarial environments
- maintain focus and cognitive clarity in complex legal work
- practise law sustainably while preserving integrity and wellbeing
- recognise and respond appropriately to signs of moral injury and professional fatigue
- exercise authority responsibly, with due regard to consequence and humanity

These outcomes support both **technical competence** and **ethical fitness to practise.**

## 3. STATE-AGNOSTIC CPD GUIDE (FOR LAWYERS & FIRMS) - HOW TO USE THIS BOOK FOR CPD PURPOSES

### Step 1 - Identify Relevant CPD Categories

Most lawyers will be able to allocate time spent with this book to:

- **Ethics & Professional Responsibility**
- **Professional Skills**
- **Practice Management**
- **Wellbeing / Fitness to Practise**

(Check your local rules.)

### Step 2 - Engage Actively (Not Passively)

CPD bodies generally require **active learning**. Suggested activities include:

- reflective journalling on ethical or professional challenges
- application of communication, listening, or focus practices to current matters
- structured reflection after complex or high-stress cases
- peer discussion or supervision informed by the Unbound framework
- incorporation of grounding and focus practices to support clarity and performance

### Step 3 - Record Your CPD

Maintain a simple record noting:

- date
- activity undertaken
- time spent
- CPD category claimed
- brief description of learning or reflection

This will satisfy most audit requirements.

# ABOUT THE AUTHOR

Dr John McSwiney is a practising lawyer and Associate Professor of Law and Business, with professional experience across private practice, government, education, and defence. His work is shaped by a long-standing interest in how professionals exercise judgment, authority, and responsibility under pressure, and how those demands affect individuals and institutions over time. While his career spans legal practice, executive leadership, and academia, a consistent focus has been the ethical and human dimensions of professional life. A significant personal loss early in his adult life led John to reflect deeply on the cost of emotional suppression and the long-term effects of operating solely on discipline and endurance. Over time, this reflection evolved into a professional inquiry: how capable, committed people, particularly in demanding professions, can sustain clarity, integrity, and purpose without erosion of self.

John's work seeks to address that question in a disciplined, evidence-informed way. As Founder and Managing Director of **Time to Transform**, he has spent more than twenty-five years working with individuals, teams, and leaders across education, government, corporate, and community sectors. His programs and publications focus on ethical judgment, reflective practice, emotional regulation, and sustainable performance, not as personal preferences, but as professional capabilities. His executive roles have included Director of Technical Training for the Royal Australian Navy, Chief Executive Officer of Haileybury International Beijing, and Director of VCAA International. In these positions, he led complex transformation initiatives at the intersection of governance, education, and organisational culture. Today, John combines legal practice with academic leadership, bringing an interdisciplinary lens grounded in law, ethics, evidence, and applied experience. His **Unbound** framework has developed into a family of books and programs designed to support professional clarity and sustainability across high-responsibility roles. His published works include:

- *The fight against 'good as' Labor Men: The Australian Labor Party and the Federal Platform 1901-1910*
- *The platform becomes law: The Australian Labor Party and the Federal Platform 1910-1916*
- *Scullin and the Great Depression: The Australian Labor Party and the Federal Platform 1929 – 1931*
- *Curtin, Labor and Total War: the Australian Labor and the federal platform 1940 – 1945*
- *Chifley and Australian Postwar Reconstruction: the Australian Labor Party and the federal platform*
- *The Journey of 100 Hidden Hearts: A Spiritual Path to your Hidden Heart*
- *Heart Unbound: The Ultimate 28-Day Heart Connection Challenge*
- *Time to Transform: Living Unbound*
- *The Unbound Leader: Redefining Leadership Through Emotional Intelligence and Conscious Clarity*
- *The Unbound Student: Building Emotional Intelligence and Resilience for Life, Learning, and Leadership*
- *Time to Transform: Living Unbound – The Evidence Companion*
- *The Unbound Organisation: Building Cultures of Connection, Courage, and Compassion*

A further work is forthcoming:

- ***A Platform Worth Fighting For: Echoes of Purpose in a New Era*** *(scheduled for publication in 2026)* A historical and philosophical examination of purpose, moral leadership, and institutional courage of the Australian labor Party and how foundational values can inform contemporary renewal.

Each publication is aligned with recognised Australian professional and educational frameworks, including the Australian Qualifications Framework (AQF), ASQA standards, the National Safety and Quality Health Service

(NSQHS) Standards, and the Australian Public Sector Capability Framework. This alignment ensures that reflective and developmental work is grounded in rigour, accountability, and professional legitimacy. Across his teaching, legal practice, and consulting work, John continues to explore the relationship between analytical precision and human discernment. He holds the view that the future of professional leadership, particularly in law, belongs to those who can sustain both: intellectual rigour and ethical presence, structure and judgment, authority and care. When not practising, teaching, or writing, John spends time in the ocean surfing and surf lifesaving, and in quiet reflection, practices that continue to inform his approach to clarity, restraint, and responsibility.

Time To Transform

EMPOWERING LIVES

Made in the USA
Monee, IL
05 November 2026

67380083R00132